Wendy —
Thanks so much —
hope you find this
helpful and inspiring —
xoxo
Ke

PERFORMING ARTS PRESENTING

From Theory to Practice

by Kenneth J. Foster

Commissioned by

Association of Performing Arts Presenters

Writer: Kenneth J. Foster, Executive Director
Yerba Buena Center for the Arts
Editor: Suzanne Fox
Art Design: Kaaryn Sanon
Publication
Development: Celia Alicata
Patrick Madden

Cover Photo: Compagnie Tchétché/Wolfgang Weimer

First Printing: January 2007

Association of Performing Arts Presenters
1112 16th Street, NW
Suite 400
Washington, DC 20036
202-833-2787
www.artspresenters.org

To order a copy of this book or obtain additional information, contact the Association of Performing Arts Presenters.

TABLE OF CONTENTS

FOREWORD

Performing Arts Presenting: From Theory to Practice **is a thought-provoking and** timely work. As the Association of Performing Arts Presenters celebrates its 50th anniversary, Ken Foster re-examines the presenter's role and offers fresh ideas for the 21st-century performing arts presenter with the same passion, candor and optimism he's brought to his own career.

There is no question that the work of presenters has become more complicated. The world has changed and we in the art world are not immune to the dramatic shifts in the political, economic and social environment. *Performing Arts Presenting* is a call to action for presenters to adapt to new circumstances, change their approach to presenting and turn challenges into opportunities.

This book resonated with me for several reasons. First, the larger issues regarding the viability and sustainability of the current arts organizational models echo findings in my work and recent national and local studies and reports. Secondly, when I was a presenter, I felt some of the same frustrations. I sincerely appreciate that a respected colleague has taken the time to explore critical issues in the presenting arena. This is a real service to the field.

It was more than refreshing to have intelligent and critical thinking examine a very broad palate of artistic work. Finally, when reading the book, I was reminded of why I first started working in the arts. My love for dance, combined with my political activism in the 1960s, led me to presenting. It was clear then, as it is now, that one path to social change is through the arts.

Moved by the events surrounding September 11, 2001 and informed by transformative performing arts experiences, Ken Foster reflects on the realities of the world and his responsibilities as a presenter to his community. No one can argue that presenters now have one of the most significant positions in the arts ecology. Ken urges presenters to consider standards of practice, new definitions and a more meaningful connection to the art, artists, audiences and our communities that will help make our work more significant.

First and foremost, *Performing Arts Presenting: From Theory to Practice* urges us to "name it and claim it"—to define more clearly who we are and what we do. Foster takes an intense look at the presenter's role and more clearly and accurately defines it. Sometimes he takes the position of the audience; at other times, he makes the case by illustrating his experiences as a presenter. He recommends a process for assessing and critically examining artistic work and introduces some refreshing new strategies for curating "classic" art, art by living artists and new cultural performances.

I, too, have felt a good deal of attention has already been paid to the management side of presenting, rather than the aesthetic framework. There are probably more than enough good books in the field on fundraising, marketing and financial management, though they will always need updating. In the context of presenting, however, there is little material that speak to the importance and value of the art and its relationship to the audience. *Performing Arts Presenting* does just that.

Ken Foster asks us to think just as creatively and innovatively as some of the artists we present to provide the best possible performance experiences for our audiences. *Performing Arts Presenting* does not suggest that an expanded presenter role is an easy role. The presenter must invest not just financial resources, but integrity and courage as well.

Performing Arts Presenting suggests a different kind of presenter for the 21st century. As Foster notes, "Presenting not just as a career, but as a calling, providing real cultural leadership." Perhaps this book will encourage the next generation of presenters. Without a doubt, it gives us a great deal to think about and question.

Not every presenter will want to or will be able to make the transition envisioned here. For those who do, *Performing Arts Presenting: From Theory to Practice* may be the 21st-century presenter's version of Abbie Hoffman's 1970 manual for survival. If so, get a copy any way you can! (Or, as Abbie would have said, steal this book!)

Mikki Shepard
Presenter, 1969—1999

INTRODUCTION

It is 2006 as I write this and the arts in America are in another of their periodic convulsions. Beset by a deeply troubled world, exhausted from three decades of turbulence in the arts, many of us are wondering not just what is next, but if there even is a next. These convulsions have probably always been the substance of our profession, but certainly they have since I entered the field of performing arts presenting in 1985.

The mid-1960s explosion of the arts in America is largely attributed to the creation and development of the National Endowment for the Arts. With the concurrent growth of state and local government funding for the arts, government support was the pebble dropped into the pond. The ripples from this infusion of resources, well documented in other places, indisputably changed the landscape for the arts in this country.

By the 1980s, when I entered the field, government support was contracting, accounting for a much smaller percentage of every organization's budget. Arts organizations were being admonished to seek support elsewhere, to diversify funding, to behave more like businesses and to embrace strategic planning, marketplace modeling and "tough decisions." Yes, mission mattered, but without money there was no mission, so money mattered more. Ever creative, arts organizations of all sizes and types struggled to find the right mix of funding to match their mission and survive. Many did and a succession of organizational models developed from the largest and most institutional to the smallest, most grassroots organizations. Each struggled to capture resources in ways that worked best for them. No one was having an easy time, but work was being created, organizations were being sustained and, in many cases, growth was occurring.

No sooner had we begun to get a grip on the economic complexity facing arts organizations in the United States when the culture wars struck. Blindsided, we found ourselves under attack, not for our lack of business acumen, but for the very art that was/is our essence. While the battle was largely played out on the field of NEA funding, which for nearly all of us had become a very small part of our budget, the real war was about cultural values, freedom of expression and the very notion of creativity in art as something desirable.

Even in this poisonous atmosphere, the economic boom of the 1990s papered over some fundamental value shifts that occurred during this time. Direct funding for artists virtually stopped in favor of funding for "safer" institutions. Risk-taking, the heart of the creative process, became deeply problematic for many institutions, which reshaped their programs to reflect a more conservative era. Experimental organizations remade themselves, contracted, folded. A generation of activists, exhausted by the struggle, simply moved on. Wherever arts administrators gathered, the conversation was inevitably about how exhausted we were from the endless struggle to find the resources to do our work. We wondered aloud what had drawn us to this work in the first place.

...the experimentation, creativity and vitality of our grassroots organizations insure an arts world in the United States that is vital, vibrant and meaningful.

Despite this ongoing struggle for money and for mission, the arts, endlessly adaptable, survived and even thrived in America. The post 9/11 economic bust that followed the '90s boom, and that to some degree persists, challenges us once again to rethink the way we do our work. We are now in what I think of as the age of collaboration, and while it is certainly no panacea, it is part of the ecological way that many of us now view the arts in America. In this ecology, we recognize that our individual health and even survival depends on the health and survival of the larger field. The stature of large institutions may serve us well in the halls of Congress and the boardrooms of America, but the experimentation, creativity and vitality of our grassroots organizations insure an arts world in the United States that is vital, vibrant and meaningful. At long last, we may be learning that we can't go it alone.

It is in the context of this ecological view that I want to reexamine performing arts presenting as an act of cultural production. In this context, I will suggest a thoughtful reconsideration of the dimensions of our work; a rethinking of who we are, why we exist and how we participate in a global cultural discourse.

Based on this reassessment, I explore specific strategies of actualizing the work of presenting in more compelling and ultimately successful ways. And of course, I examine the role of the individual presenter and how each of us can truly achieve the full potential of being a performing arts presenter.

But I begin with a few stipulations.

First, I suggest that it is past time for our field to fully accept the idea of "performing arts presenter" as not just an activity but as a defined, named profession. Years of skirting this assertion by allowing ourselves to be identified as arts administrators, theater managers, sponsors, curators and other such terms has meant that we have failed to acknowledge the full complexity of performing arts presenting. Each of these terms stands for an aspect of our work; only together do they begin to describe the profession of performing arts presenter. By failing to embrace this more complete understanding of our role, we have failed to accept our impact in the world. We have also failed artists and audiences by not being as courageous as we must be. We can no longer believe that anyone with access to a theater and a box office who "books shows" is a presenter. Instead, it is time to recognize what is demanded of us aesthetically, intellectually and morally as arts presenters and do a better job of meeting the demands of the profession, the arts ecology and the world.

Second, I acknowledge that while I will be speaking to the whole field, I primarily will address the segment whose work is institutionally situated and the individuals who run those institutions. This is the segment that most needs to reconsider its work. Our failures as institutional presenters can result in promoters, amateurs and dilettantes assuming our role. While much good can come out of freewheeling circumstances, it doesn't change the fact that the ecology suffers from our shortcomings. So I am particularly advocating a strengthening of this part of the arts ecology. A study conducted in 2001 by the Urban Institute on behalf of the Association of Performing Arts Presenters ascertained that there were approximately 6,000 presenters in the United States, serving more than 300 million people annually with thousands of performances and a gross revenue approaching $5 billion.[1] Clearly, presenters hold in their hands a giant piece of the arts ecology and the very cultural heart of America. It is to them this book is directed.

---

[1] Mark A. Hager and Thomas H. Pollak, *The Capacity of Performing Arts Presenting Organizations* (Washington, D.C.: The Urban Institute, 2002), p.43.

Some see presenters in an agency role, pulling the levers of power on behalf of artists in a market-based system that is, in fact, anathema to the artistic process. I don't share this belief, though I recognize where it comes from and the validity it has. What interests me more is developing a deeper understanding of the role of the presenter. Although I would argue that much healthy change could occur in the worlds of the artists, the managers and the funders that would dramatically improve the arts ecology, these arenas are generally outside the scope of this work.

Finally, a work such as this is clearly the product of my own experience. Having worked for more than twenty years as a performing arts presenter, with ten years of service on the board of the Association of Performing Arts Presenters, I have had the unique privilege of meeting and working with an enormous range of people, many of whose thoughts and ideas inspired my own, causing me to either reaffirm what I knew or rethink what I thought I knew. I've been inspired by the 1989 report of the National Task Force on Touring and Presenting, *An American Dialogue*, a work which transformed many peoples' understanding of the field and how to work in it. And I have lived and worked through a period of immense change in our field. So what follows are my own thoughts, synthesized through the lens of my particular experiences.

It is my hope that this book can be the beginning, not the end, of a dialogue that I believe needs to occur in our field, a dialogue that will enable us to achieve a more thorough understanding of who we are, recognize the vital importance of what we do, and develop strategies to achieve our full potential as a field. With that, we can assert ourselves, our work and our profession as the vital part of the arts ecology that it must be.

◆ 1 ◆

UNDERSTANDING PRESENTING

SO WHAT IS THIS ACTIVITY CALLED PRESENTING?

At a workshop of arts presenters I once attended, a facilitator asked the participants to recount their first "meaningful arts experience," i.e., the first arts encounter that they could recall that imprinted on them indelibly the love for the arts that ultimately propelled them into a career in the field. The responses ranged from singing in the church choir, to being bused with their class to an orchestra performance, to participating in high school theater, to dancing with and for their friends. Of particular interest was the manner in which individuals responded to this question. Initially hesitant to reveal something so intensely personal, most began wearing their "slightly bored, slightly engaged, slightly distracted" workshop faces. Soon into their stories, however, people relaxed. In many instances, they took on the demeanor they probably had at the very moment of the experience being related. Clearly every person in the room had, at some point, been fundamentally changed by an arts experience. While some could articulate their reactions, many could not, lapsing into clichés and wordlessness.

What started out as an ice-breaker for a workshop experience became a marker of the human condition, a sign that even among arts professionals who strive for a dispassionate relationship to their work, deeply emotional and even spiritual responses to works of art do occur. Art changes lives in ways both profound and personal. The transformative ability of art rests at the heart of the presenter's work.

Presenters are also inveterate observers of audiences. In my pre-presenting career as teacher/theater director, I realized that as I created and performed, I simultaneously observed the audience. How were they responding? Was I making sense? Was the point being made? How effectively? Did I have them? Was I keeping them? Did I lose them there? Why? What happened? The interior monologue of a theater director at a performance or a teacher in a classroom is often of this nature, and as the performance continues, the critique happens simultaneously. In the best of all possible worlds, the creative process allows for repeat performances so the critique can inform the work and the work can become more powerful as it evolves in response to the audience.

For many years, my thinking about presenting has been focused specifically around this duality of purpose—caring deeply about what happens in the art and what happens to the audience—and recognizing this as the core of the presenting endeavor. The presenter introduces new forms, and new art reaches the community. Audiences are drawn into the performance space through effective marketing and carefully considered strategies of audience development. The presenter is engaged in the act of connecting art, artist and audience. While this is not the most complete description of what happens through the art of presenting, I still see it as the fundamental work of the presenter.

In looking at the field more widely, I see a range of both thought and action around the practice of connecting art, artist and audience. One type of presenter might think almost exclusively about the audience, to the neglect of the art itself. In this practice, what happens on stage is secondary to the audience being there and having a good time. Numbers mean success. The larger the audience, the more successful the event.

At the opposite extreme is presenting which offers an uncritical platform to artists. These are the instances in which the artist may or may not be engaged in a substantial and important endeavor, but is simply following a creative impulse and playing to an audience of devotees. The circularity of response between artist and audience is a closed loop, admitting neither new audiences nor new ideas. As long as funding can be found to support this endeavor, it continues and is also judged a success by its practitioners.

Each of these extreme examples, as well as the more common middle ground, has a claim to the rubric of performing arts presenting. After several years of observing this phenomenon, I became increasingly convinced that this "anything goes" nature of the field was not necessarily a strength, as it is often described. Rather, I came to believe that lack of definition allowed an increasing amount of activity and resources to be directed to endeavors that we called presenting but that did little to advance the field, support and sustain artists or assure healthy presenting activity in the arts ecology. I began to worry about this and wonder how it could be changed.

In the early 1990s, I started serving on the faculty for "Presenting the Performing Arts," a workshop of the Association of Performing Arts Presenters (Arts Presenters) in which inexperienced presenters came together for a week in the summer to learn the basics of their newly chosen or newly found profession. Teaching this workshop required me to struggle with the fundamentals of our profession. Working with a wide array of colleagues helped me explore multiple perspectives about what presenting is and how we approach our work.

A few years later, when Arts Presenters asked me to revise and rewrite the curriculum for the course, the full dimension of the challenge I faced became clear. Some parts of the course, which had been taught over several years by knowledgeable and experienced presenters, organized themselves with ease. The practical ideas of marketing, fundraising and other management issues required only my organization of what had already been done. But I kept encountering the essential questions of what were we doing and why we were doing it. I realized that no organized thinking, no writing, no precedent around questions of purpose had emerged that I could arrange into a teachable pattern. It struck me then that this was not a problem for me alone, but one for the field. Over the next several years, I became interested in trying to put some structure to this amorphous idea of understanding what, exactly, performing arts presenting is.

I thought about the artist, especially during and after the culture wars of the early 1990s, and the need for the presenter to support the creative process of the artist in multiple ways. I thought about the individuals in the audience and the ways their lives were changing. I thought about the phenomenon of the audience as an entity and the power of presenting to create, shape and affect that entity. I embraced the audience development concept in which the presenter became a truly engaged member of the community, taking arts presenting to a new level of civic responsibility. All of these ideas became part of my growing recognition of the complex, multi-faceted endeavor of presenting the performing arts.

Interestingly, the events of September 11, 2001 and the immediate aftermath galvanized my thinking. Through my own work, I recognized explicitly what we were really engaged in as performing arts presenters and I became motivated to articulate these understandings to the field.

September 11 was four days before the opening of the 2001-2002 season at UApresents, the arts presenting program at the University of Arizona in Tucson of which I was Executive Director at the time. On September 15, we presented "The Sprit of Cambodia." This evening-length performance of classical Cambodian music and dance was organized by The Asia Society, The National Dance Project and the New England Foundation for the Arts after several years of working with the Royal University of Fine Arts in Phnom Penh. That was extraordinary enough, but the context for the work made the performance especially significant. During the time of the Khmer Rouge in Cambodia, as the government sought to excise the debilitating effects of western civilization and the corrupting effects of modernity, artists and intellectuals were specifically targeted for extermination. In a way that most of us can hardly imagine, a people set out to exterminate its own culture. And it nearly succeeded. Eventually, the Khmer Rouge regime was deposed and the Cambodian people began trying to both survive and reconstruct their society.

"The Spirit of Cambodia" illustrated the reconstruction of culture that had been accomplished post-Khmer Rouge. It gave western audiences a brief idea of both the struggle and the result. It revealed the beauty of the art and the problem of saving a largely oral tradition, passed down in practice from teacher to student. It also showed us the courage of the people and their determination to preserve their culture. It was a graphic depiction of the power of art and the will of a people to continue under the most unbelievable circumstances.

At the performance that evening, the theater was very different than usual. Those who attended were subdued and even anxious. A palpable sense of unease filled the crowd, as did a simultaneous desire to come together, perhaps to experience a bit of normalcy in a world that had suddenly become disturbingly abnormal.

As Executive Director, I knew that I had to make a public statement before the performance. Our organization was deeply engaged in both the work of the artist and the life of the community, so we knew that it was important that we provide context for the evening. We had never experienced the combination of the enormity of the events of September 11 and the enormity of the art we were to present that evening. Speaking from the stage just before the performance, I briefly described the political context of the Cambodians' work, drawing a parallel to the circumstances we now found ourselves in. I said, "Their struggle, their courage and, as you will soon see, their triumph, are a testament not only to the power of art but to the strength, the resilience and the indomitable spirit of a people. It is our collective hope that through tonight's performance we will be reminded of the power of art to heal, to replace despair with hope, sadness with joy, grief with understanding and compassion and a desire to celebrate what is most magnificent about the human spirit."

Dance-The Spirit Of Cambodia/Rachel Cooper

For two hours that evening, about 1,000 unnerved Americans shared space with the courageous artists of Cambodia in an unforgettable experience, one in which the threads of connection between the spirit of Cambodia and our own situation became abundantly clear. I realized that, as the presenting organization, we had played a critical role in making the experience happen.

A week later, we presented Ali Akbar Khan in a performance of classical north Indian music. At 78, Khan is an acknowledged master of the sarod; his depth of skill and understanding in interpreting Indian classical music is legendary. Performing in America, he has adapted the form for western audiences, who seem incapable of sitting still through an entire raga and aesthetically unable to follow the intricacies of this music, which provides an opportunity for meditation and introspection.

Once again, I was to make a curtain speech. By now, post-September 11 shock had set in and the dark side of the internal war against terrorism was surfacing, including placing Arabs, certainly, but often any person of color in the United States, into the category of potential terrorist. In nearby Phoenix, an Indian-American, going about his daily work as a gas station owner, had been murdered by a white American. Air travel was still restricted and the now-commonplace searching and screening of travelers was still relatively new. Khan and his entourage drove to Tucson from the Bay Area to avoid potential harassment while flying. It was extraordinary that they were even there. In my speech, I referred to the work of the Cambodians the previous week, briefly described the journey of Khan and his musicians by car from San Francisco and concluded by saying, "A performance of North Indian classical music depends on the inspiration of the artists and their rapport with the audience. I have no doubt that we will find in tonight's performance by these singular artists, the courage, the strength, the solace and the hope that we long for at this time, and that these artists know that this is their gift to us and to the world."

Khan began the concert with a series of short pieces that were accessible to a western audience before closing the first half with a longer piece that began to fully explore the possibilities of his music. The audience response was fascinating—restlessness during the first accessible part, increasing attention during the latter, longer, more difficult piece, as if they were seeking something more. After intermission, he returned to play a raga that took the entire second half of the performance. A palpable sense of both internal meditation and person-to-person connection flowed through the audience that evening, as Khan's music touched some deeply spiritual place within us. The moment of silence at the end, followed by an explosion of applause, signaled to me our collective experience of a profound sense of peace. Once again, as the presenter, we were a catalyst for an extraordinary experience.

One month and several varied performances later, the Japanese drumming group Yamato took the stage. By now, pre-curtain speeches had lost their point. A sold-out audience filled the hall expecting both something different and something approaching normalcy in their lives. We had experienced the courage of the Cambodians who had come to us with their message of survival at a time when we desperately needed it. We had shared a spiritual experience with Ali Akbar Khan who had provided us with an extraordinary meditative opportunity. We now had Japanese Taiko drummers who promised spectacle and virtuosity. Somehow it made sense at the moment.

As the performance began, I observed the audience. I saw then how entirely right this company was at this time for this audience. That night, the artists provided an evening of pure celebration. The performance took us beyond spectacle and beyond virtuosity to a place of deep joy. Once again, in this theater, this sacred space that was the site of profound, transformative experiences, an extraordinary event occurred. For two hours, we did not escape the resonance of September 11, but we did find a moment of joy through tragedy that all human beings long for. In a way different than the Cambodians and Ali Akbar Khan, Tucsonans that night found strength, courage and hope when all of these seemed in short supply. Once again, the presenting organization had created a transformative experience.

In a unique way, these events served as a post-September 11 catharsis for our community. And while I have described the particular experience of my own organization and my own community, I know from talking with colleagues across the country that such occurrences were created by presenters everywhere. In many cases, presenters, like other arts organizations, understood instinctively the need to serve as a community rallying point and as the focus for a community's fear and grief. It is true that some performances were cancelled because of their apparent unseemliness at a time of national mourning. But many more went on as scheduled, testifying to the courage of the artists, the audiences and the presenters. Each event created, contextualized and actualized by a presenter explored depths of feeling that were both appropriate and necessary.

...presenters, like other arts organizations, understood instinctively the need to serve as a community rallying point and as the focus for a community's fear and grief.

In our case, these particular artistic expressions demonstrated vividly the global connection that had simultaneously brought us the despair of September 11 and the path toward healing. At this devastating historical moment, how could we possibly claim a disconnection from the rest of the world? How could we not see clearly the need to engage in cultural dialogues that illuminate so much to us and about us? If, at a particular moment, classical Cambodian dance became a transformative experience in the life of people in Tucson, Arizona, what other possibilities exist for transformation if we are deliberate about creating them?

At the heart of all performances, of course, is the work of the artists. What these events taught me, however, was that the work we as the presenter had done to develop the audience, the efforts we made to contextualize the experience, the guidance and support we provided to the artist and the audience, ensured, in every case, that a profound experience could occur. No doubt the events of September 11 created a uniquely powerful resonance for the work of the artist, but without the work of the presenter, that resonance, had it occurred at all, would likely have had a greatly diminished effect. An opportunity for a transformative experience would have passed us by.

Our experience with art and artists post-September 11 is neither unique to that time nor to the power of art in any time of human tragedy. History is replete with examples of courageous artists performing during repression, during totalitarianism, even during genocide. We know that at the most desperate times, art, not politics, not economics and not military action, creates within us the courage to face a world gone mad. That inspirational courage for all of us is driven by the courage of the artists and, importantly, by the courage of presenters as well.

I now saw that through our work, presenters can inspire a complex series of transformations. The individual's response to the art and the artists is at the center of an experience that extends to the audience, is presented at a specific moment of time and is situated within a specific community. These multiple layers of transformative experiences, I believe, can come together to transform the world.

Presenters therefore must think more deeply and profoundly both about what actually happens at this moment of transformation and what role they play in making that experience happen. Only then will we recognize the vital importance of our work and fully embrace our responsibility, as performing arts presenters, to the world.

•2•

CREATING THE PERFORMANCE EXPERIENCE

TRANSFORMATION BEGINS, OF COURSE, WITH THE PERFORMANCE ITSELF.

A few years ago, I accepted an invitation to a contemporary dance festival in Europe to immerse myself in a form of contemporary dance that had not been particularly accessible to me. The trip involved meeting and talking with many artists, choreographers and artistic directors. I hoped this experience would help me find a way to approach the work and better learn to appreciate it.

It did not quite work out that way. The artists I saw and spoke with were, with few exceptions, immersed in the dilemmas of their artistic lives, those angst-ridden moments that are played out in dense, cerebral, unapproachable and, at least for me, often uninteresting work. I started leaving performances before they ended, something I try never to do no matter how uninvolved I am in what's happening onstage. I became increasingly frustrated with the entire experience.

On the last day of my time at the festival, tired and discouraged, I searched for something different. I found a company from Africa that was appearing in a small performance space. Since I'd had virtually no experience with contemporary African dance, I was intrigued, believing that, at the very least, it would be a change from the work I had been viewing. I decided to take a chance.

A handful of us sat in what was clearly one of the least desirable spaces of the festival venue. Sitting in bleachers with no backs in a "black box" environment, with no backstage area to speak of, we watched the performers make last-minute preparations. The lights dimmed, musicians appeared and the performance began.

What happened in the next forty minutes can only be described as transcendent. Accompanied by music both plaintive and powerful, four extraordinary women came into the space. Their physical appearances, while varied, conveyed a palpable sense of internal strength. They took us on an unforgettable journey into their experiences, their hearts, their souls and the soul of their country, Cote d'Ivoire. Moving powerfully through the space, they performed a dance of anguish and of love. Their bodies made contact, pulled apart and then came together again and again, embracing, slapping, falling and catching each other, reaching for a depth of connection and even love. Through their dance they revealed anger, pain and betrayal, the depths of which we can only guess at as they touched, caressed, beat on and held themselves, each other, the floor, the space, the music. And us. With breathtaking rapidity, they made their experiences ours as much as theirs. As the work came to an end, the entire audience felt the depth of their strength and their will to survive. We understood their need to dance, to dance in order to live. Like them, we were, by the end of the piece, overwhelmed. There was nothing to be done but to hold, breathless for a moment, and let the emotions pass through us before rising. Tears streamed down everyone's faces—dancers and audience alike. We, the audience, tried, vainly, to touch them back with our applause as they had touched us. With our cheers, we refused to let these shamans, these magicians, leave the sacred space they had created moments earlier.

...even though performance is specific and unique to the moment, it reverberates beyond that moment, changing the direction of lives and events well past the performance and extending to individuals who, in fact, were not even there.

The company is Tchétché, which means "eagle," and is based in Cote d'Ivoire. It is composed entirely of women under the artistic direction of Béatrice Kombe, a visceral and visionary choreographer. This piece, "Dimi" explores both the struggles of women in Africa and the strength required to confront those struggles. Sitting in that small, darkened space, I was transfixed by the performance in a way that nothing else in the festival had done. Despite my state of mind when it began, despite my lack of context for this company and this piece, I, and indeed everyone in the audience, was profoundly transformed by the experience.

Since that time, I have had several occasions to describe this experience to others. Each time, when I reach the moment of attempting to explain what occurred within me at that performance, words fail me. I struggle to explain and I cannot find the language to adequately describe the experience. Only those who have had a similar experience with art can begin to understand it.

It was, I believe, the complete performance experience.

What really happened here? What elements came together to create this indescribable response? Was my experience in fact not singular, but shared by the rest of the audience in the theater? Did their presence there influence my own experience? And what of the reverberations of the performance? If I say I was "transformed," how does that play out in my life following the performance? How were we brought together for such an experience? And can it be repeated?

These questions, and others like them, begin to approach what I believe rests at the heart of the work of the presenter—the creation of the performance experience. Presenters should be concerned with the totality of that experience. The core of the experience is certainly the connection the artist makes with each individual in the audience, a connection that will vary in scope, meaning and dimension with each separate individual.

But the performance experience is also communal, characterized by a connection both among the members of the audience and between the artist and the audience as a discreet entity. Finally, and no less important, the performance experience can and does extend beyond the boundaries of time and space, affecting both the specific community within which it occurs as well as, potentially, a larger regional, national, even global community. Paradoxically, even though performance is specific and unique to the moment, it reverberates beyond that moment, changing the direction of lives and events well past the performance and extending to individuals who, in fact, were not even there.

The art of presenting, then, is centered not around the production of art but rather around the creation of the performance experience. This complex activity demands the presenter's attention to the art, the artists, the audience, the immediate community and the larger context of culture and the world. To really work, it requires of us a deep understanding of every facet of the performance experience and the role the presenter plays in making this happen.

What do presenters need to know and do to create and sustain this experience? To answer this question, we need to look first at the performance experience itself and the role of artist, art and audience in creating that experience. Next, I think it's important for presenters to understand more thoroughly what happens within the performance experience—to the individual, the audience, the specific community and the global community—to fully appreciate the impact of our work. If we understand more thoroughly these components of the performance experience, a new understanding of presenting inevitably emerges, one that is more expansive than we previously may have thought.

Once we recognize the importance and the complexity of what we do, it follows that we should reexamine the way we each engage in this work. We must look carefully at ourselves and our relationship to art, artists and community to attain a more complete understanding not only of our responsibilities as presenters, but also of what is required of us to fulfill that role to the highest degree. With these new understandings, we will be better equipped both to create profound performance experiences and to fully appreciate the purpose of the presenting enterprise.

The Art and the Artist

Understanding the performance experience begins with the art, its creation, its interpretation and its performance. Art begins with the artist's creative impulse and is manifested through the artist's chosen performance medium. This part of the creative process, while vital to the presenting endeavor, is largely outside the scope of the presenter's work. The presenter may work to facilitate and support the creative experience but, in fact, the artist creates the art.

Crucial for presenters, though, is an understanding of the process of art-making as well as a critical facility around the performing arts. In doing their work, presenters must encounter hundreds of artists to find those that can create meaningful performance experiences. Inevitably, this requires not only seeing countless performances, but also making aesthetic judgments about those performances. This process, central to the presenter's curatorial function, is a multi-faceted endeavor with its basis in craft but its realization in areas well beyond virtuosity.

The core of the art-making experience is craftsmanship. Regardless of the medium, the artist must demonstrate the ability to effectively and excellently wield the tools of his or her chosen artistic endeavor. Watching artists warm up before a performance or take a company class or work through voice and movement exercises, one sees that craft is as much a daily challenge as it is the springboard of creativity. Great artists devote their lives to refining their craft. Even artists who are masters in their field will admit that, while the structure of the learning process may have changed, they still work on their craft. They recognize it as the bedrock of their work and the process that will carry them through an often-grueling schedule of rehearsal and performance. For presenters, the presence of craft consistently on the stage is the first line of demarcation between those artists who may be able to create the performance experience for our audiences and those who cannot.

When Tchétché performed, the craft was immediately discernable. The training of the dancers was completely evident in their bodies and in the physicality, power and virtuosity they brought to the choreography. One could imagine few other dancers who could execute the movements as these dancers did. Structurally, the arc of the dance was concise and well designed. The music and the movement intertwined and built to a powerful climax and an affecting denouement. Superb and thoughtful choreography supported by a specific movement aesthetic was brilliantly executed. The power of the piece began with its craftsmanship. Since making judgments about craft is a primary challenge for presenters, it requires extensive experience with the art. Ideally, presenters are, or have been, artists themselves and therefore have an understanding of the art-making process. Alternatively, they are lifelong students of the arts, developing their critical abilities through extensive study of and experience with many different performance experiences. In either case, the ability to distinguish the authentic from the false, the skilled from the sloppy, the innovative from the derivative, the virtuoso from the pretender, deserves the full attention of the presenter.

Compagnie Tchétché/Wolfgang Weimer

But craft alone, no matter how superb, will not create a transformative performance experience. A presenter in search of the art and artists most likely to create transformation must push his or her artistic judgments beyond craftsmanship. The presenter's thinking about art should encompass multiple aesthetic considerations and include a full exploration of the work itself and the complex range of possibilities inherent in its relationship to the audience. As a way of positioning that thinking, I propose four questions that can bring the presenter closer to understanding what happens in great art and which can serve as the basis for critical examination of performing arts.

Is There an Idea, an Intellectual Basis to the Work?

What idea is embedded in the work that can be discussed, analyzed, argued? Meaningful art will cause the spectator to rethink previously held assumptions. Arguably, one can distinguish art from popular culture on the level of intellectualism. Sheer entertainment, diversion, does not challenge the intellect. It exists simply to wash over its audience, perhaps to make them feel good in the most superficial of ways. Art makes people think.

The more complex and profound the questions the artist explores, the more likely the performance will reach depths that also profoundly engage the individual audience member. Questions of human psychology, social injustice, cultural relevance and the very idea of being human are at the root of many of the most profound artistic experiences. These are not simple questions and they do not invite facile responses. Rather, they are subjects that artists have always explored and will continue to explore. Because they are fundamental questions of human experience, they invite investigation. Through art, we seek insights, at least, if not understandings.

During the Tchétché performance, while not a single word was said, a choreographic idea which contained an intellectual inquiry was clearly present. What is the status of women in this society and why? What is the source of their oppression? What part do we play in that oppression? What are the reasons for their sorrow? Béatrice Kombe, the choreographer, was able to open up these and related ideas through the medium of dance. The audience found it impossible to attend the performance without considering these ideas, and even more impossible to leave and forget about them.

Does the Work Provoke Emotion?

If the artistic dialogue were centered solely around an intellectual idea, one could argue that a rigorous discussion of the ideas themselves might be much more intellectually satisfying than a performance. And indeed that could be the case, should the desire for discourse remain centered at a purely intellectual level. But the artist chooses the medium of performance out of a need to explore an idea beyond the intellectual level. Emotions, which define the human experience, also define the performance experience. The depth of emotional content can vary across the full range of human emotions; extremes such as anger, sorrow and joy are likely to be remembered and remarked upon. Most importantly, the power of emotion is what inspires the artist to create. That same power inspires audiences to repeatedly attend the performing arts in search of the full performance experience.

The emotional content of Tchétché's performance distinguished it from much of what I had seen at the festival. Creating moments of sorrow, rage and courage in the face of adversity, the dancers seemed possessed by their emotions in a way I don't always find in contemporary work. The awareness of both the strength of these emotions as well as the raw way in which the dancers inhabited them made the piece incredibly powerful and emotionally overwhelming. The audience's response testified to its emotional substance.

These three components—craft, idea and emotion—create extraordinarily satisfying arts experiences. A substantial amount of the work that shows up on presenters' stages is described and assessed in this way, and this is not a bad place to be for the art, for artists and for audiences. But at least two other aspects of art and art-making contribute to the presenter's ability to create transformative performance experiences.

What is the Spiritual Component of the Work?

While emotion may reach the human heart, spirituality reaches the soul. Art can do this as can no other medium. A spiritual dimension to a work of art requires that the art simultaneously take us outside ourselves and deeply within ourselves, connecting us with a sense of the infinite that is intangible, yet, on some level, knowable. The performance becomes an experience in which we recognize that sense of the infinite and understand ourselves as part of something larger than ourselves. It works on the deepest recesses of our being in ways both private and public, humble and extraordinary. It reminds us that we are human even as it enables us to aspire to something beyond our humanity. It is life-changing and soul-enriching.

The spiritual connection to the art that occurred immediately after the Tchétché performance remains for me now, several years later, as transcendent as it was then. I, like others at that performance, had a moment that took me within myself but also outside myself. The deeply human quality of these women, the shared pain and sorrow that we felt, the indescribable human connection, left me feeling not just part of their world—a feat in itself—but part of a larger human universe. To experience the indomitable human spirit, to sense kinship and connection among strangers, is to know, through a performance, a spiritual experience.

Is the Performance a Thing of Beauty?

The concept of beauty is even more rarely addressed in the presenting world than the idea of spirituality, despite its centrality to the creation of art. How should presenters define and discuss beauty, a concept that has been the subject of volumes of thought and discussion by philosophers for centuries? The challenging nature of the question should not prevent us from considering art in the context of its ability to create beauty.

I think of beauty as the coming together of all of the previous elements to produce a sublime experience. The individual components of beauty may vary dramatically, encompassing classical form, raw emotion, extraordinary craft, profound idea and more. Beauty exists in the aspiration to the ideal, in the striving of imperfect humans toward an idealized concept—inevitably we fall short, but we achieve grace in the struggle. Artistic form may be the structure within which beauty is created, but it may also be the standard against which beauty is created by deviation, by its willingness to subvert the conventional ideal in favor of the deeply imperfect and ultimately human expression. Beauty is a concept as much as a reality, a process as much as an outcome. However presenters recognize it, it can and should be a critical element of their thinking and understanding about art.

Was there beauty in the performance of Tchétché? I think so. Working within a contemporary dance vocabulary, the choreographer and the company created a work of extraordinary grace. It successfully blended exquisite form and profound content. All of the elements of design and craft worked together to create an intellectually, emotionally and spiritually satisfying work of art. "Dimi" also showed us the transcendence inherent in human imperfection, in the passion of individuals and the enactment of their deepest desire for something greater. Bringing all this together created a work of extraordinary beauty.

The performance experience, then, begins with the creative impulse, which is translated into a physical form by an artist. It springs from highly developed craft and a considered idea, exploring the essential questions of humanity. It embraces emotion, incorporating and subsuming the deeply personal experience of the artist, the creator and/or the performer. This deeply personal expression helps us connect to the work on a visceral level. But finally, the work plunges into the unknown. It takes us—artist and audience—to places previously unvisited, to a spiritual realm that touches our souls. In so doing, a work of extraordinary beauty is created.

The Audience

While the performance experience begins with the art, the presence and participation of the audience is a second critical component of the experience. The very essence of the performing arts is a shared experience between artist and audience. The audience member, the receiver of the art, ultimately creates meaning for the performance. The presenter therefore plays a particularly important role in bringing the audience to the experience. Understanding the audience as thoroughly as the art becomes the second component of the presenter's effort in creating the performance experience.

Understanding the audience as a whole begins with seeing them as individuals. While the presenter strives to understand the audience as a collective entity, that understanding begins by recognizing the individual, what the individual brings to the performance and how individual backgrounds and experiences can affect the performance experience. I propose six components that are key to the presenter's understanding of the audience.

The Individual's History and Psychology

The life experiences one carries into a performance unavoidably affect the experience for both the audience member and the artist. Contemporary America has become both proficient and prolific in exploring the individual psyche. We recognize that individual Americans experience and internalize a range of experiences from the most sublime to the most horrific. This recognition allows for the possibility that the psychological depth brought to the artist's creative act is matched by that of the audience member. This creates the potential for a psychological collision that can define the performance experience.

How self-reflective a person may be about his/her life varies, of course. The self-help and therapeutic industries have encouraged many to explore their experiences, a process that is vital to the arts. Only if we are willing to psychically engage the artist's craft, intellect, emotionality, beauty and spirituality can we create meaning through performance. In the performance itself, the interaction that occurs is defined by the art and by the individual psychology of the audience member. Artists and arts presenters have cause to be optimistic because many Americans seem prepared to engage their psychological lives in a performance setting, creating opportunities for transformative arts experiences.

An Ability to Consider an Idea

A second component of what the individual audience member brings to the performance is the ability to both recognize and seriously consider an intellectual idea, especially one that challenges him or her to move beyond a personal known to an unknown. Like the individual psychologies present, the intellects are certain to be different. For many, intellectual training has centered on analysis rather than exploration of ideas. This can present a singular challenge for the artist and the presenter who are interested more in questions than answers and who need their audiences to follow that line of inquiry as well.

Individuals who are accustomed to exploring new ideas are deeply invested in the creative process. They understand the thrill of exploration and the joy of discovery. They appreciate the beauty of form and are inspired by the creativity within it. They have contemplated serious thought and are often eager to engage on a high level with artists who are also doing so.

Those individuals who are more analytical tend to be mostly interested in trying to "figure it out" and seek recognizable narratives and explanations for "what is going on." The socialized emphasis to "get it" has, in fact, dampened the desire of many to explore and discover. This attitude, which may seem to be the prevailing one about intellectual inquiry, can be frustrating for presenters who are trying to introduce new art and new ideas to their audiences.

Still, we have reason to be optimistic. A fundamental curiosity exists, I believe, in virtually every individual. The presenter and the artist can work together to connect to that curiosity in multiple ways. Certainly this is not easy work, but presenters must resist the tendency to "give them what they want" and instead seek out opportunities for audiences to explore the edges of their knowledge and understanding. This is as true for form ("What is modern dance?" "Why should I care about contemporary music?") as for content. It makes the challenge of presenting one that requires the creativity and innovation of the presenter as much as the artist. It also requires a sustained investment of time, resources and work.

Arts Education or the Lack Thereof

The typical American's lack of general knowledge about the arts is most often cited (and blamed) for a host of ills related to the performing arts. For more than a generation, the decline in arts education in the public schools has shaped the potential arts audience. Most audiences possess neither a common vocabulary about, nor shared experience with, the performing arts. The diminution of arts education has also placed the arts in a secondary role in our culture. It should be no surprise, then, that the description of the arts as "a frill" is still common. Nothing in the education of most Americans contradicts that assumption.

Nevertheless, arts education for our children occurs in many forms, some of which are not connected to formal education. We have a plethora of after-school programs, private dance academies, private music lessons and other child-based social situations devised around creating and performing art that comprises a distinctively American arts education. Nor do we often acknowledge, as we should, the influence and importance of street art—music, theater and dance created outside the parameters of formal settings or school-based arts education models. Rising from people's need to express themselves through performance, such art can be just as powerful and transformative as formal performances—sometimes more so. Some individuals, often young and from marginalized communities, have never had a place in the formal art world, but may have a very specific and highly developed arts vocabulary, understanding and appreciation. Presenters are challenged to make this informal arts education work for their programs.

An Individual's Capacity to Respond Emotionally to Art

Presenters need to acknowledge the varying abilities of audience members to respond emotionally to a performance. Some people allow themselves to engage with the performance experience on an emotional level and allow the performance's emotional effect to touch them. Best of all are those willing to also allow themselves to publicly express that emotion.

Others will resist steadfastly any emotional or psychic tugs. These individuals remain emotionally unaffected or, if they are moved by the performance, they are often unable or unwilling to express that emotion in public. Since performances are distinctly public events, this presents a particular challenge for presenters. While we acknowledge the audience as a collection of individuals, we strive for them to achieve a spirit of oneness in the performance experience. Presenters can, however, work to create that spirit of oneness, both in the way we talk about the performance to the public and the specific strategies we use to create the audience. A "dead" audience often says as much about the presenter as it does the artist.

Social and Cultural Background

Besides understanding the individual and his or her ability to engage with art, presenters must also consider the social and cultural backgrounds that people bring to the performance experience. Here, too, the range of experiences is quite extraordinary, even daunting—the social and cultural values an individual brings to the performance are as varied as his or her psychology. Presenters have to understand the social and cultural history of the United States if they are to fully understand the community in which they are working. Presenters must educate themselves about the varied histories of community, nation and world as well as the situations that have arisen from that history and thus gain perspective on the background an audience member may bring to the performance experience.

Issues of immigration and race in particular underlie the social and cultural history of the United States and demand sustained examination and attention. Understanding the United States as a nation of immigrants means recognizing that no single or even primary national aesthetic exists. The results of the 2000 census dramatically illustrate that America continues to change at an astonishing pace. The cultural shift that started in the 1960s continues with explosive growth in immigration from non-European nations. The increase from 1990 to 2000 of 31 million immigrants, fully 80 percent from Asia, Latin America and Africa, indicates the most extraordinary socio-cultural shift in the nation since the beginning of the 20th century.[2] Happily for presenters, these new immigrants come from countries and cultures in which the arts often play vital roles.

This cultural shift creates enormous opportunities for the presenter. It allows for the critical reevaluation of the role of the arts in a nation in the throes of a dramatic sociological shift. The performing arts have become a hugely open field of choices, aesthetics and experiences, all legitimate and all derived from some aspect of our shared values. We should be far less interested in creating artistic hierarchies of importance and value and more committed to the diversity of artistic expressions that can now become part of every presenter's work.

The reality presenters face is that the social values and experiences of individuals in their potential audiences differ radically from one another. Similarly, their experience with specific art forms also varies dramatically. It follows then that no art form exists or can be sustained simply because "it should." This may

---

[2] The Census Bureau website www.census.gov provides an extraordinary amount of both local and national population change data derived from which these numbers are drawn.

be a challenge for some presenters, but one that carries with it an important opportunity for creativity and a better chance for the presenter to create transformative performance experiences.

Spirituality and Spiritual Values

Finally, the place of spirituality and spiritual values also has shifted dramatically over the course of the past century. Recognizing and understanding the nature of that shift is equally important for presenters, particularly as some individuals turn to the arts for the spiritual sustenance they may not be receiving anywhere else.

The United States has long been, and continues to be, a nation steeped in organized religion. The role of religion in our society is well documented and its power remains strong. But communities are not monolithic and presenters should resist the characterization of their communities into a specific religious persuasion. The proliferation of alternative spiritual paths, journeys and awakenings is truly one aspect of the American character. The search for meaning through alternative practice has been countered, however, by the increasing visibility of religious fundamentalism. Presenters will likely find within their communities people who are deeply suspicious of new spiritual paths to enlightenment as well as those who are seeking spiritual sustenance outside of organized religion.

The implications for presenters are both profound and challenging. As organized religion has asserted itself even more strongly in the political realm, presenters find themselves confronted not only with artistic challenges, but also political challenges. While we should of course remain aware of political realities, we cannot back away from our commitment to creating transformative arts experiences, ones that push the boundaries of the known in startling, often dramatic, ways. Presenters must demonstrate their courage as well as their commitment to the expansion of, rather than the constriction of, the human spirit, even if, or perhaps because, it challenges religious orthodoxies.

So where does this analysis of our audience take us? We find that as a population, we do not share a universal set of experiences, understandings, cultural values or even language. If the individual audience member is as vital to the performance experience as the art and the artist, are we then reduced to a closed loop of niche artists performing for niche audiences, separated by art form, cultural background or spiritual belief? I hope not. I believe instead that presenters are now challenged to adapt their thinking, their planning and their presenting to the multicultural, multi-experiential audience that is the reality of contemporary society. If we begin there, we can set about the complicated but exhilarating task of creating the performance experience for a new American society.

◆3◆

DECONSTRUCTING THE PERFORMANCE EXPERIENCE

The Experience of the Individual

For the individual, the performance experience is about the creation of a new reality.

At the moment that art and audience member connect, a contemporaneous reality is created, one that exists for that moment under the very particular and carefully designed circumstances of the performance. In the best performance experiences, something far more profound than "the willing suspension of disbelief" occurs. The audience member is transported, released to the care of the artist, taken on a multi-sensory journey that completely engages the intellect, emotions and spirit. This is a moment of intense humanness, at which the individual feels not only present and connected but also alive and aware, even hyper-alive and hyper-aware. It can be a sublime experience, a moment of such perfect beauty that we crave its recurrence.

Crucial to the multi-dimensionality of the performance moment is that the audience member has not lost touch with reality, is not hypnotized nor in a trance. Often, in fact, the individual is acutely aware of the immediate surroundings, functioning easily in the twin realities of the performance experience and the environment in which it is being created. Conflicting ideas may be sorted, ordered and discarded; connections are made and links are established between the twin realities. Time becomes a fluid commodity ("I had no idea two hours had passed!") as the mind races, engaging with the past, the present and the future.

The desire to reflect intellectually and to thoughtfully articulate the idea of the performance piece is strong. It may be several moments, hours or even weeks before the intellectual process is complete if the performance experience has raised questions rather than provided answers. The ability to live with those questions, to tolerate that level of ambiguity, is an important human trait. Over time, the spectator intellectually accepts a revised reality created by the performance, one that confirms, changes or even deconstructs what we thought we knew.

Emotionally, the performance moment can also deeply affect us. Often a performance uncovers and releases repressed feelings, emotional touchstones we have stored in inaccessible parts of our psyches. The performance experience will often help us find those feelings. In some cases, only through the performance experience do we even allow ourselves to express an emotion, recognizing that the vicarious reality grants us permission to act and react in unusual ways. Open demonstration of tears or laughter, joyous celebration with those around us, pain and sorrow too deep and too profound to be expressed or shared even with our closest confidant—all these can and do find their places in the performance experience.

Performance creates the opportunity for a spiritual experience as well, that recognizes our connectedness on a higher plane of understanding. We may be only intuitively conscious of it at the moment. Only later do we attempt to describe or characterize the experience and even then we realize that we may not have the words to explain the depth and totality of what we have experienced. Yet we know our lives have been fundamentally altered by this encounter. This is why we will return to performances repeatedly to re-experience (even if we sense that it can't be recreated) this moment of spiritual awareness.

The theater, the concert hall and the performance space have been described by artists as spiritual places. Originating in many cultures from sacred spaces designed for worship, they have been adopted and adapted for what we acknowledge are secular performance experiences. Nonetheless, the ability to create spiritual experiences remains within all performance spaces and with the artists and audiences who come together there. Presenters must work assiduously to create the sacred spaces and spiritual experiences that define the performance experience.

The Communal Experience

Understanding the full dimensions of the performance experience is not complete if the presenter focuses solely on the interaction between the artist and the individual audience member. Both the artist and the presenter are also deeply concerned about the audience as an entity and are interested in how that entity responds to the performance. Conversations between artists and presenters following a performance are often about the response of the audience. How did they react? Did they react at all? What feeling did the artist and the presenter have about the audience? Over time, both presenters and artists begin to characterize audiences at performances and even venues in general terms—they are a "good" audience, a "dead" audience, a "smart" audience, a "knowledgeable" audience.

This conversation centers on attempting to understand and describe exactly what happened in the performance space. While we implicitly acknowledge the interaction between artist and individual, we are particularly focused on the more encompassing group dynamic of the audience. This experience is critical to a successful presentation; after ticket sales, it may be the most discussed evaluative criteria in the field.

> Often a performance uncovers and releases repressed feelings, emotional touchstones we have stored in inaccessible parts of our psyches.

The communal experience is the connection among the members of the audience during a performance. The presenter recognizes that both the communal experience and the individual experience are key to the successful performance experience. They are co-dependent experiences which require each other to define themselves. Indeed, the overriding effect of the performance experience is the webbed relationship among the audience, the art and the artist and the ways in which the actions, thoughts, feelings and responses of each affect those of the other. Taken together, a uniquely shared performance experience is created, one that can never exactly be replicated. Without the individual's response to the art, there is no possibility for a connection between art, audience and artist. What crucially distinguishes the performance experience from other artistic experiences is the ability to connect simultaneously to the other individuals in the shared space.

Most arts enthusiasts can recount in some detail the really awful experiences they have had in a theater or concert hall when audience behavior or its very existence has deeply disrupted the individual's experience. But most arts attendees can also recount experiences in which the presence of the audience not only illuminated the experience but also enhanced it. The audience created such a singular moment that the event itself became completely memorable as a communal experience.

While I have been lucky enough to have had several such experiences, one of the most accessible was at a performance of the Broadway musical "Dreamgirls" in 1982. From the moment the performance began, the audience was a single entity. Shouting to the performers, talking back to the stage, commenting on the story as it progressed, the audience helped create a community between itself and the performers. I returned several weeks later in search of a repeat of this experience. This time, with a very different, more reticent audience, a very different, subdued and, frankly, less satisfactory communal experience was created. The performance quality was perfectly adequate, seemingly as professional as before, but the communal experience was vastly different.

At the heart of the performance experience remains the desire of both the artist and the audience to connect in real time with the real people assembled there. No matter how artists manipulate their performance through technological means, no matter what degree of inconvenience the audience endures to arrive at a specific time and place, the fundamental concern of both still rests with the performance moment and its communal, as much as its individual, characteristics.

Habib Koite/Stefan Buggs

The presenter plays a pivotal role in creating the communal experience. The role encompasses not only the logistics of presenting, but also extends to the selection of artists, curation of a season and development of an audience for the performance. Indeed, most artists would concur that the presenter's chief responsibility to the artist is not simply producing a large audience but one that connects with the artist and with one another.

At UApresents, we presented a concert by the Malian artists Omou Sangare and Habib Koite that illustrates this point well. For this performance, we confronted an increasingly common issue—in our traditional theater, we had to be prepared for people to stand up, to dance, to approach the stage. These were key components not just in enhancing the individual's experience with the concert but in creating the communal experience we desired.

The audience entering the theater represented what we had come to recognize was typical of world music concerts—a core of people from the artist's homeland amid a broader spectrum of our community, people from multiple races and ethnicities, ages and socio-economic classes with highly varying degrees of familiarity with the artists or even Malian music in general. From the moment that Habib started playing, I was caught up in observing the nonverbal communication among audience members. Right from the start, a few people stood up and started moving to the music. Recognizing that they were blocking the view of those around them, they quickly moved to the aisles. Seeing both the space to move, and the permission granted by the courageous few who began the exodus to the sides, others joined them. Soon, the aisles were packed with people moving, dancing, clapping, cheering to the music. The majority of the audience remained in their seats but nonetheless included those who were dancing into their own experience of the concert. An exuberant and joyous experience was created not only between artist and audience but also among audience members.

After intermission, Omou Sangare, the queen of Malian music took the stage. She also played to the crowd, but her set took on a very different feel as she began pulling men up on to the stage to dance with her while she sang.

Of course, for the presenter, this is a moment of both great joy and great fear. We were thrilled at the connection between artist and audience but fearful of what might happen to the equipment, to the band, to the artist and to the audience member. Visions of liability lawsuits danced in my head. It was not a moment of complete pleasure. Should we get them off the stage? Stop the show? Stop Omou? Is any of this possible, or desirable?

In the few moments that these thoughts occurred to me, the solution appeared. After dancing briefly with "the queen," the men left the stage of their own accord. They were clearly thrilled by their contact with this legendary woman and aware that it was to be only a moment. Toward the end of the concert, as the excitement was reaching its peak, a young Malian man leaned against the wall, tears streaming down his face. "Thank you," he said. "Thank you for bringing her to Tucson. I am from Mali and it is such a joy to be here tonight and hear this music." He was at the center of a community that had been created that night, by a presenter, with an artist, around a performance experience.

Creating the communal performance experience is not limited to performances that allow and encourage an audience to have physical and verbal communication with the artist or to dance in the aisles. It can occur just as regularly in an art form such as classical Western European art music, which has completely different audience-artist expectations.

Classical music has unspoken rules, understood by the experienced attendee but rarely, if ever, articulated. No unwrapping candy, no clapping at inappropriate moments, no talking, no vocal expressions of any sort are allowed at what is primarily an auditory experience. Any behavior that interferes with that experience is prohibited. One is to remain completely still in the seat. Offenders are punished with disapproving looks, stares and even, from time to time, verbal reprimand. Attending a classical music concert seems meant to be an interestingly solitary experience performed in public. The intent is rapt attention and intense concentration on the music, to establish a one-to-one connection with the performer and the music, despite the fact that the event occurs in a public place.

Good presenters make every effort to accommodate these listening conditions for this audience. In the 2000-2001 season, UApresents presented a Beethoven Quartet Cycle—six concerts by three different quartets of the complete Beethoven string quartets. It was a major undertaking; advance ticket sales were quite strong and the chamber music lovers of Tucson were out in force for what they all anticipated would be an extraordinary experience. But the first concert, by the Emerson String Quartet, did not begin well.

The lights dimmed and the quartet entered to applause. Bows were raised; the quartet waited for the perfect moment to begin what we all hoped/knew would be a transcendent experience. A collective silence of anticipation filled the hall. A fraction of a second before the ensemble was to begin, a volunteer usher entered from the rear with a latecomer. Unaware that the moment to seat was long past, he started down the aisle with the patron, a young woman. Phil Setzer, playing first violin for the Emersons, held his bow in abeyance. It became clear the woman was seated close to the front. A second more and it became clear this would not end quickly; the quartet put their bows and instruments down. The usher continued down to the very front row with the patron who by now was the focus of the entire audience. At the row, which was filled except for one vacant seat, the usher stopped to examine her ticket for what seemed an eternity. Finally, Phil Setzer gestured to the vacant seat in front of him and said in a loud voice, "It's down here."

While many laughed at this moment, many did not. Several people muttered angrily at this breach of etiquette, not just on the part of the patron for arriving late but also at the presenter for not having adequately trained the ushering staff about the etiquette of classical music performance. It was an excruciatingly painful moment. But it was also a moment of collective experience that, in a strange way, united the audience as a single entity. Even those who were less offended by this intrusion on performance practice still recognized it as a spontaneously human moment, shared by artist and audience.

The performance experience that followed pushed the opening incident into the recesses of the audience's minds. The quartet played sublime music with extraordinary feeling and the connection between audience and artist was felt, if not seen. Caught up in the performance, the audience literally breathed along with the performers. There were moments of such profound connection among the audience members and between artist and audience that the pauses were filled only with silence. No doubt, even without the opening incident, such a transcendent experience could have occurred. But the incident itself illustrated the fact of a community existing within the performance space. And in a strange way, it made the outcome, the performance, even more exciting than it would have been otherwise.

Emerson String Quartet/Mitch Jenkins

The implications for the presenter are clear. Presenters exist not simply to serve the artist, though that is an important aspect of our work. Nor do they exist simply to create the conduit between artist and audience, critical though that work is as well. The presenter works to bring together artist and audience for a communal, performance experience. While this seems unlikely or even impossible within a social construct that allows any given individual to elect to attend the performance or not, the presenter in fact exercises remarkable control over how the communal experience can be actualized.

The context that the presenter creates for the performance is fundamental to the experience. Is this the most appropriate presenter to present this particular artist, or would the performance experience be better served by another organization, more sensitive to the needs of the art and more connected to the potential audience for the art? The context also includes considerations such as the appropriate venue for the performance, not simply for the artist but for the audience as well. Should financial considerations drive chamber music into increasingly large halls? Should music events that will stimulate audience movement and dancing be presented in venues that do not allow for those? How welcome (or not) does the potential audience feel at a particular venue? All these issues are under the control of the presenter and all have an impact on the performance experience.

Contextualization also can be created by the information that the audience receives in advance. It should do more than introduce the artist and provide a synopsis of the work to be performed. What can the audience expect at the performance? Beyond the parameters of etiquette that concern presenters and audiences alike, what degree of intellectual, emotional and spiritual engagement can one expect? Are the circumstances of the presentation such that these responses are encouraged? Will we be allowed to express emotion? How? What new knowledge can the presenter provide in advance that will allow the audience to connect more deeply to the performance than an uninitiated spectator might? The presenter must consider these and dozens of other issues to create a fully contextualized performance experience. The goal is to cultivate an audience that is prepared not just to attend the performance but also to experience it fully. Who shows up and how ready they are to approach the performance should not be a matter of pure chance. Instead, the composition of the audience should be a conscious creation of the presenter.

The logistical implications of this responsibility are also the work of the presenter. Presenters know that the temperature in the hall affects the experience. So do the sight lines and the seats. The experience the audience member had getting to the hall, buying the ticket and finding the seat affect the performance. The level of expectation that the presenter has created can work for and against the experience, depending on what finally happens onstage. And presenters are acutely aware of the limitations they have on many aspects of this experience, including what kind of day an individual might have had before coming to the concert.

But if presenters care deeply about the communal experience, as they should, then they need to think carefully and deliberately about it from the very beginning of the curatorial process. It requires examining our own experience with the performers and their ability to serve as the core of the performance experience. It also requires a knowledge and awareness of our potential audience and the degree to which reaching the moment of communal experience is even possible. In an alienating and isolating society such as ours, creating a communal performance experience is challenging. Presenters are often dealing with communities and audiences who rarely engage in meaningful communal experiences.

But just as presenters must strive to reach the individual's need for a profoundly spiritual experience with the arts, they must also seek to fulfill the individual's need to have that experience be communal, a deeply felt human connection with a group of people, many of them strangers, who come together to collectively celebrate human creativity and the joy of the live performing arts at a given space and time. Performing arts presenters have an opportunity to make sure that our diverse culture retains its ability to come together in a shared and sacred space.

Community Engagement

We have seen that the heart of the performing arts experience is the vital connection between the audience member and the artist. We know, too, that an inherently communal experience is intrinsic to the performance experience and that the presenter can construct that communal experience. But the performance experience also has a resonance beyond time and space. Performances, in fact, occur in a deeply contextualized world and while most discourse around performance occurs concurrent with the performance itself, or shortly thereafter, we should recognize the effect of the performance beyond that moment, as well as its impact on the community and even the world.

The nature of this impact can be seen in the individual life experiences of the artist, the presenter and the audience member. Because our lives are linear, the performance experience contributes to our ongoing narratives, becoming a notable event in each participant's life history. The transformative nature of the performance, however, extends its reach beyond the real time constraints of the performance moment. The performance becomes part of each of these individual narratives and also changes those narratives, affecting the future life and development of each person—artist or audience—engaged in the specific experience.

For many artists and presenters, an urge to create change in the world is their reason for creating the performance experience. If the performance is indeed a transformative one for those who attend, it follows that the transformation of the audience members also becomes a sociological event. The reverberations extend beyond the time and space of the performance, from the specific individuals, through the audience as an entity, out to the community and to those who did not attend the performance but are still affected by the thoughts and actions of those who did.

This idea has been manifested repeatedly by artists whose primary aim is to illuminate a social issue and propel individuals to respond actively to it. If nothing else, artists hope that their cogent and insightful expression of the issue will cause the individual audience member to reevaluate and review his or her own actions, ideas and politics. Extend this idea to multiple performances, and especially to artists who tour, and the opportunity to create a nationwide or even worldwide movement of activism becomes not only possible, but feasible. A community of individuals dedicated to social change is created within the general community, the nation and the world.

Understanding the cultural transformation that occurs through performance, however, means looking deeper than overt political or social activism to a richer and ultimately more powerful performance experience. Since meaning in performance is created by the audience, every performance becomes an open text, subject to interpretation and, ultimately, some type of activation, by the audience member. What happens after the performance experience—how the audience member and the artist have changed and how that change reverberates through the community—is even less under the presenter's control than the experience itself. In a certain sense, the artist and the presenter conspire to lob phenomena (art) into a controlled situation (the performance setting), but they can only observe the effects of the phenomenon they have created.

Recognizing this even if they do not articulate it, some presenters choose to support artists whose ideas placate rather than disrupt audiences. These experiences also affect the community, if only to reassure or, at worst, anesthetize a public. Other presenters may choose to create artistic experiences specifically to provoke disruption throughout the community long after the performance ends.

The crucial points for the presenter to recognize are first, that the resonance occurs with every performance presented, not just the "controversial" ones, and second, that here too, the presenter is responsible for constructing the community's experience. A presenter whose season is filled with banal and diversionary events is responsible for creating a banal community, irrespective of who or how many people attend the performances. A stimulating and provocative program that provides audiences the opportunity to reassess their values and beliefs creates a similarly thoughtful and engaged community. Content matters, and it especially matters in creating opportunities to challenge the audience's thinking. In some ways, the number of people attending actually matters somewhat less since the reverberating effects of every performance ultimately affect the entire community. The question for the presenter then centers on the types of experiences to create. In this construct, the artistic choices that a presenter makes take on a much more significant meaning than the presenters might initially realize or even want to acknowledge.

Extending this idea to performing arts that tour, it becomes clear that presenting can create new national and even international communities of individuals who have explicitly shared a performance experience, albeit in different locations, and been transformed by it. Again, the performance event reverberates through these multiple communities, and the widespread effect is so broad and so deep that fundamental cultural change occurs. That change extends even to the individuals within those communities who did not themselves attend the performance.

Last Supper at Uncle Toms Cabin/The Promised Land/Jeff Day

Examples abound of the effect of the presenter's work on the community culture. Often the effect is articulated in economic and quality of life terms as presenters become involved with, and critical to, a community's vision of itself as culturally active. Presenters who have been in a single community for a long time are best able to see the fruits of their work. They can point to a shift not only (or not even) in the amount of performance activity but in the evolution of the audience, and its ability to engage with more complex and provocative work. The effects of this play out differently in different places, but the presenter's work is a crucial component of a community's ability to define and redefine itself.

A vivid example of this phenomenon was the presentation in 1990 of the Bill T. Jones Arnie Zane Dance Company epic work, "Last Supper at Uncle Tom's Cabin/The Promised Land." Loosely based on the Harriet Beecher Stowe novel, the work explores religion, racism, homophobia, personal spiritual beliefs and social constructions in the United States. A large-scale, full-evening performance, the piece also required the local presenter to find about 30 people of all races, ages, ethnicities and body types, to perform in the work with the company, a performance that, not incidentally, obliged all of these performers to appear nude onstage.

The aesthetic of the work was one thing, but the community it created within the performers was another. Individuals, many of whom were not trained dancers, rehearsed with the company and coalesced as a unique community. The community created within the audience was, of course, part of the experience, as were the experiences of the communities that embraced the piece through the work of the presenter. Importantly, however, the community of presenters engaged in presenting the work became the catalyst for a uniquely created national community. The meanings created by the performance reverberated within each community and, through the network of presenters, across the nation.

The community building began with the challenge for the presenter to develop a group of individuals willing to participate. For the presenter, who lived in the community and would remain there long after the performance was over, assembling these people could be an arduous task. It required articulating someone else's vision of the work, since it was not the presenter's creation. The presenter may have seen some portions of the piece in workshop, but, especially for presenters early in the tour, it was very much a matter of describing a work-in-progress. Presenters could talk generally about the themes of the work, about Bill T. Jones and his work, what might happen, the logistics of the two-week rehearsal process, and the remarkable final segment which required nudity from all the performers, but often not much more than that.

...the community of presenters engaged in presenting the work became the catalyst for a uniquely created national community.

Over the course of the preparation year, the presenters who had signed on held meetings with Bill to discuss the implications of the project. Those conversations raised numerous issues for the presenters about their own racism, homophobia and fears of extending themselves beyond the safety of administrator to producer. For presenters, a leap of faith was certainly required—artistically, managerially, financially and, in most cases, personally. Bill made it clear that he intended to challenge the presenters as much as himself, the performers, the audiences and the communities.

The weeks leading up to the performance were exciting, exhilarating and terrifying. Many presenters encountered community or organizational resistance to the idea of the piece, including the idea of a stage full of naked people, most of them from the local community. Press interest was high and that took its toll on presenters, who were constantly explaining, contextualizing and clarifying what this performance was about and why it was important to their community. Interaction within the community was widespread and deep. It began with the performers themselves, some of whom thought they could manage the work but ultimately decided they could not. There were all the predictable issues of getting so many disparate people together to create a work of art. In short, most presenters found themselves at the center of a maelstrom, which may not have been typical of their previous experience.

The results of the performance experience were, of course, different in every community, but in every case, the performance was transformative. In many of the host sites, a project of this scale and complexity had simply never occurred, nor had many of these communities been part of a national dialogue the way that this piece demanded. The discourse that followed was often contentious and confrontational; individual reactions to the work were always intense, regardless of where they were on the aesthetic or social consciousness continuum.

What made this particular performance experience exceptional was not just the breadth of the experience nor the numbers of people involved. It was that the experience forever changed most of the participants, communities and presenters. Bill was as demanding of the presenter as he was of his company, the local dancers, the audience and himself, and that demand extended to the immediate communities and the network of communities nationwide. Determined to engage a national audience in a process that stretched comfort zones around a whole host of relevant issues, he devoted his vast creative energies to a nationwide project that remains one of the seminal artistic and community engagement works of the late 20th century.

An experience such as this clearly demonstrates the important role of the presenter in creating a site of cultural dialogue and community engagement. Through performances, presenters are instrumental within their communities, and even nationally, in provoking discussion and action around important issues. The discourse may be around social issues and causes, but it is just as likely to be centered around exploring and understanding the human condition. The role of the presenter in creating cultural discourse includes the necessity to elevate both the role of the arts and that of the presenter beyond mere purveyors of entertainment. Art clearly matters, and not just to artists.

Recognizing this significant role of the presenter fundamentally alters the way that any presenter envisions the organization and approaches his or her work. It raises questions that responsible presenters cannot ignore. As the performance experience breaks the boundaries of time and space, it takes on a life that extends backward and forward and is not situated in a given geographical place. Inevitably, the dialogue spins out of the control of the presenter and the artist. This is not only acceptable but desirable. The ideas take on lives of their own, carrying the discourse in unexpected directions. This cultural anarchy becomes a moment of great excitement and potential and deserves to be supported and nurtured by presenters and their organizations.

Nurturing freedom of expression means accepting that the event is likely to be messy—noisy, uncontrolled, unregulated and, at the same time, deeply enriching and exciting. The noise inevitably creates mistakes, misspoken assumptions and a kind of intellectual and emotional chaos. The presenter must both stimulate and support this chaotic experience to allow the individual spectators and community members to find their own ways through competing ideas, ideologies and expressions. Much of what was said by all kinds of people during the "Last Supper" experience was overblown, out of control, not always well thought out. Ultimately, however, the experience uncovered ideas, emotions and beliefs that defy control and rationality. We see the ability of art to create change within us; we don't always acknowledge the power of art to create change within the community. Yet this is the power of presenting and it requires unstinting courage and support to flourish.

The performance event as a site of community engagement incorporates the realities of the ordinary individual's life within the discourse of the arts. The juxtaposition of the artist's creative impulse with the community of the moment creates an energy that is at the heart of the performance experience. When these two worlds collide, the results can be astonishing. The perspective that the community brings to the world in which it lives may conflict dramatically with the perspective of the artist, whose work allows him the privilege of seeing through lenses both more sharply focused and more broadly encompassing. Change begins at the moment that these points of view intersect.

Presenters see this intersection of perspectives all the time, often in an audience's reaction to expectations met, or not met. We see the discovery process of an audience, the surprise when the artist delivers what the audience was unprepared for, the laughter, the anger, the fear, the disappointment. All these emotions are a function of the art meeting the audience and the synthesis that occurs then.

The opportunity for the performance event itself to attract and meaningfully engage a broad range of people is extraordinary and should be central to the presenter's work. The collision between the artist and the audience cannot occur if the predictable artist is performing for the predictable audience. A cultural dialogue and the opportunity for transformation are more likely to occur when participants have different perspectives. The subsequent alteration of idea and ideology occurs within this construct. Presenters must have as part of their mission the charge to create circumstances in which audience members approach each event with a context of "informed openness," a spirit of discovery or inquiry. This approach is vital not only for individual transformation but also for a community to be created and transformed through art.

The collision between the artist and the audience cannot occur if the predictable artist is performing for the predictable audience.

Community transformation occurs when the presenting program attains its rightful place as a site of cultural dialogue. Failure to make this an inclusive experience that provokes a cacophony of points of view and artistic expressions means the marginalization not only of the presenting program but often the art form. Classical music is perceived as elitist; contemporary dance is seen as incomprehensible; new music is dismissed as dense and accessible only to a few aficionados; so-called ethnic work is suitable only for that ethnicity. These points of view marginalize the art, the artists and the presenting program as outside the stream of community life. This marginalization creates two negative effects. One is that a void is created and becomes filled with the most mundane "art" because it at least has the ability to be comprehensible to "most people." The other is that important art forms struggle to survive and are limited in the more vital quest to grow, develop and expand.

The presenter must be responsible for connecting the art to the community; for insuring that a site of community engagement is created and sustained and that all art forms, properly contextualized, enter the cultural dialogue. Equally important is that the full range of audience perspectives are introduced into the performance experience. In so doing, presenters create the opportunity for transformation. The vitality of both performance and presenting, as integral to the community's identity, are thus insured.

The recognition of the power of the arts to influence and change whole communities, within and outside of the performance experience, was at the root of the culture wars of the 1980s and 1990s and led to the deliberate effort of those in power to do whatever was necessary to shut down the anarchy of the arts experience, lest it spin out of control. Legislators believe in the necessity of legislation to control human behavior. Art, fortunately, defies legislation. As long as the anarchy was confined to a small group of people (the so-called arts community), there was less concern. But as the arts, including arts presenting, decentralized and became integral to every community in the nation, fear became widespread. Certainly a multiplicity of causes and ideologies were at work in the culture wars, but more than anything else, they were a response to the democratization of the arts and the recognition that art changes lives. Presenters, unwittingly sometimes, were and are at the center of that transformation.

The Global Discourse

In the global context of the 21st century, the presenter's responsibility for creating the performance as a site of cultural discourse takes on additional importance. In the discussion around globalization, what it means and how it is occurring, the conversation is usually couched in economic terms, political considerations and, most recently and most devastatingly, military actions. The discourse about globalization and what that means for the individual, communities, cultures and nations plays itself out almost exclusively in a military-political-economic framework.

A conversation about how globalization affects art and culture is usually missing, even though artistic expression is both inherent in cultural understandings and vital to a society's ability to navigate the contemporary world. If a cultural dialogue emerges at all, it tends to be around the hegemony of American commercial culture worldwide and the deleterious effects of the corporatization of art. While this important topic is worthy of discussion and debate, it hardly encompasses the totality of the dialogue that is needed. Aesthetics, spiritual meaning and understanding, rituals, signs and symbols and their resonance for individuals, communities and specific cultures are largely absent from the global discourse.

Many of the seemingly intractable issues that confound the world are rooted in conflicts about deeply held beliefs and understandings. Political, military and economic disagreements and the confrontations that follow result from these conflicts—they do not cause them. Solutions are sought at the military, political or economic level that fundamentally fail to address the root issues of cultural conflict. It becomes crucial then for the contemporary presenter to take on the responsibility for creating cultural dialogues and engaging their communities in the larger conversation.

Simply presenting work from other countries is only a superficial response to this situation, though it is a place to begin. Even at such a low level, however, the presenter must create appropriate context for the performance that elicits respect, understanding and awareness rather than misconceptions or alienation. Respecting the integrity of the work and translating it appropriately for American audiences is a complex and important aspect of the presenter's responsibility to the cultural dialogue.

When we focus on the performance event as a site for a global cultural dialogue, opportunities arise that can fundamentally shift the dialogue and place art and culture at the center of the conversation, rather than at the margins. What works of art demand to be presented at this particular moment? What possibilities exist to create circumstances in which the art may provoke dialogue and lead to better understanding of different points of view? How can the performance experience create transparency around culture and difference rather than further density and opaqueness? How presenters respond to the challenge of the global community has consequences not only for the arts and the community but, indeed, for the world.

Inevitably the question arises about the presenter's desire to engage in a cultural discourse at all. It is more comfortable, or perhaps simply safer, for the presenter to avoid the implications for community engagement. Is it not possible for a presenter to simply present art, to create strong seasons of great art for people who want to see that art and find it a pleasant, even engaging experience, and leave it at that? Must every presenter be engaged in "changing the world"?

Whether intended or not, every presenter is engaged in changing the world. The arts ecology created in any given community (and it is created, it doesn't "just happen") gives that community a vivid and defined sense of culture. What that looks like will vary from locale to locale; the presenter plays a primary role in determining what the outcome will be. Major cities may feature a broad spectrum of work from non-profit and commercial presenters and producers. The responsibility of creating a cultural dialogue rests with every one of these arts producers and presenters, even if they resist the notion. A city in which commercial entertainment dominates will create a cultural reality for that community that is very different from one in which a broader range of more thoughtful or provocative work abounds. (Think Las Vegas versus San Francisco.) Cities that invest heavily in "major institutions" are dependent on them to create a wide-ranging program that speaks to, and is reflective of, the wide range of cultural expression in the country and the world. They may be up to this task, but often they are not—often they are defeated by their very institutionality. In a large and diverse city, the presenters and artists with fewest resources and much more at risk are often producing and presenting the work that stimulates the most radical social and cultural change. Only later is it reflected in the aesthetics and work of the larger institutions.

Smaller cities and rural areas may rely more heavily on the presenter to be the primary organizer of performance and therefore the focus of cultural dialogue. In these circumstances, the presenter carries even greater responsibility. The presenter becomes the window to the community's sense of the world and an important component of its understanding of itself. Especially in smaller communities, the presenter cannot avoid this responsibility. The only variable is the integrity that the presenter brings to the work.

The performance experience remains one of the few vital places of engagement in the contemporary world, in which we can take up the challenges of both transforming individual lives and entering the global discourse. Presenters carry significant responsibility for creating such experiences. Artists are engaged in articulating what is in their hearts and souls. Audience members must navigate through complex messages and stimulation for understanding and insight. Presenters have both the means and the responsibility to create, through the performance experience, the chance for minds, hearts and souls to come together in a moment of extraordinary power.

◆4◆

REDEFINING PRESENTING

UNDERSTANDING THE MULTIPLE DIMENSIONS AND CONSEQUENCES OF THE PERFORMANCE experience requires that we think differently about presenting. We know that performing arts presenting is an important part of the American arts ecology. An entire industry has developed that has at its center connecting and audience. Especially for art forms like modern dance, most music that is not symphonic, interdisciplinary work, experimental work of all types and even some theater, a presenter is required so the art can reach the audience.

This structural circumstance has resulted in ongoing dialogues within the field about terminology and identity, especially as the role of the presenter has expanded. Is a presenter the same thing as a producer and, if not, what is the difference? Can a presenter simultaneously serve as an artist manager? How does that affect the work of presenting? While these questions are interesting to contemplate, they do not address the fundamental theoretical issues about the role of the presenter in the contemporary world. How an individual or organization defines itself, especially since those roles are often multi-faceted, seems less relevant. What is relevant, however, is understanding and exploring the complexities of presenting and its impact on the arts ecology. In so doing, presenters are challenged to think more deeply about their work.

Presenting Redefined

Historically, the role of the presenter has been that of facilitator: selecting the artists, hiring the theater, advertising the performance, selling the tickets and then moving on to the next project. Today, most presenters understand this as the most rudimentary definition of presenting, although elaborating on this role often results in simply filling in more details of what is essentially a mechanical function. While presenting undoubtedly incorporates these functions, the true nature of presenting is more than facilitating.

The core function of presenting is to design the performance experience, the moment at which the art, the artist and the audience intersect. Certainly this requires a fully developed collaborative relationship with all of the parties, but at the heart of the endeavor is the presenter.

Designing this moment is a creative act. It does not just happen and, most importantly, it does not happen in an environment free of the aesthetics, values, beliefs, ethics and background of the individual presenter. As a creative act, the presenter's role becomes quite a bit more complex than it might seem initially. Defining presenting therefore requires a more nuanced and multi-layered conceptualization than it has generally been given.

In creating the performance experience, presenters should recognize their role as translators. Translating involves serving as a mediator; contextualizing the work so that audiences can receive it more thoroughly and more thoughtfully than they might otherwise. Contextualization involves everything from the most concrete operational details to the more conceptual work of how (and why) the presenter selects the performances and talks about the work with a potential audience. The presenter should think carefully and comprehensively about all the actions that must be undertaken to insure that the performance experience is meaningful for the audience. This is a vastly more complex task than simply connecting artist and audience.

There are some who believe that the presenter's translation function is an unnecessary impediment, a barrier, in fact, to the undiluted connection between the artist and the audience member. This is especially true for the aficionado who knows the artist, has experienced the art form and thoroughly prepares for the performance experience. Such people are increasingly rare, but even their performance experience can be enhanced by the translation of the presenter. And since the performance experience is communal, any given individual's experience will depend greatly on the composition of the audience. Finding and developing that audience is an important part of the presenter's work.

Like any translator, the presenter's function is to make previously inaccessible work available to a larger audience. Few would disagree that it is preferable for art to be made available to a larger public rather than kept as the exclusive domain of the select few. Viewing the performance experience in the larger context of community engagement only magnifies the importance of the presenter's role as translator, since it recognizes the importance of bringing diverse cultures and points of views to a broader public.

Beyond translation, the presenter's work extends to that of the creation of meaning with the audience. Meaning in performance is created at the moment of interaction between artist and audience, when the artist translates a creative impulse into a performance and the audience member translates the performance experience into personal meaning. As the steward of the audience's experience, the work that the presenter does to contextualize the performance becomes critical to how the audience receives the artist's work. The first step in this process is for the presenter to work hard to find those artists and performances that possess the strongest potential for creating meaningful arts experiences.

This role places the presenter in a complicated relationship to the art and the artist. The presenter faces an often unacknowledged but continually present conflict of serving the art while simultaneously being distanced from it. This paradoxical relationship is necessary to carry out the challenge of creating meaningful arts experiences. The presenter must simultaneously be of the field and independent of it, knowledgeable and aware of artists and their work while still passing judgments that are centered primarily on the content and aesthetics of the work. Those presenters who already question their own abilities to understand art have enormous difficulty here. Their critique is less rigorous and the opportunities for creating meaning are consequently diminished. At the same time, it is neither necessary nor particularly desirable for the presenter to assume the role of iconoclast, even though originality and innovation can be attributes of an excellent presenter. A presenter pursuing a specifically personal aesthetic agenda misses his or her central obligation to create the performance experience for an audience. Presenters must strive to retain both independence in relationship to the art and a connection to the audience.

Profound experiences are individual and personal, private exchanges between artists and audience members, but presenting performances is a public act, which leads to another aspect of the presenter's role—creating a cultural discourse. When the presenter brings together many different artists and performances, profound work that explores the complexities of contemporary life creates a dialogue among various points of view and insights. Even if the works are of varied genres, time periods or styles, the opportunity exists for the presenter to allow the community to participate in the contemporary cultural discourse.

This discourse occurs on multiple levels. It certainly occurs on an internal level as individual audience members compare their thoughts, ideas and beliefs to an artist's new vision of the contemporary world. Indeed, the power of art that endures rests in the ability of the audience member to revisit it and discover fresh insights each time. Similarly, the discourse occurs on the socio-political level, and it is important for presenters to acknowledge that every season makes a socio-political statement to the community. It is disingenuous of presenters to pretend otherwise and to see themselves as outside the socio-political discourse of the community. It is equally disingenuous to view only overtly political work as having political or social content. Even the most unimaginative presenting program participates in the political discourse by its very lack of provocative ideas. Creating a cultural discourse requires the presentation of multiple ideas and points of view, or there is no possibility for dialogue.

When the presenter brings together many different artists and performances, profound work that explores the complexities of contemporary life creates a dialogue among various points of view and insights.

Context requires that presenting be seen in a national and international perspective. It is naive and even irresponsible for a presenter to maintain that "my little series of events" is somehow localized to the point of being outside the international discourse. The mere presence of international artists, who may be exploring different ideas than domestic artists, makes one statement. The absence of such artists makes a different one. The curatorial dialogue among the artists on a presenter's season begins the participation in the global discourse. This becomes even more important in smaller and more remote communities, where access to a broad range of art and artists is more limited. The responsibility of the presenter to create cultural discourse increases exponentially, the further the presenter is from more cosmopolitan locations. Indeed, the apparent divide in the United States between the values of the "red and blue" states can arguably be seen as a consequence of the absence of a sophisticated cultural discourse created by presenters in their own community.

It logically follows that the presenter's role in shaping the culture is another aspect of presenting. Shaping the culture is not the same as creating it, which is the province of the artist. Because the presenter controls much of the infrastructure of the performing arts, however, the art that the community experiences rests largely in the presenter's domain. Presenters play an important role in determining which art gets moved forward, which receives the imprimatur of both excellence and importance, which art and artists will survive and thrive. Consequently, presenters play a vital role in determining what art will define us as a people.

One of the most recent and obvious examples of this phenomenon is the increasing presence of hip hop and street cultures in performance spaces and presenting series. Unquestionably, hip hop artists were creating culture through their work long before it was "discovered" by so-called mainstream presenters. Yet by bringing this art to their stages, presenters have helped shape the culture of the nation, just as they did when they began to move jazz from the clubs to performing arts centers. In both cases, an "alternative" art form emerged that, largely through the work of presenters, has redefined mainstream American culture. Again, presenters cannot take credit for creating these art forms, but they have been important to fundamentally transforming American cultural identity through bringing marginalized art forms to a wider audience.

This facet of performing arts presenting places important responsibilities on the presenter, requiring extraordinary research and understanding of the arts. It requires a commitment by presenters to endlessly expand their artistic horizons and to seek and find the makers of culture who are working in both traditional and non-traditional places. It also requires artistic rigor from the presenter, to be able to distinguish the trendy from the important, the fashionable from the meaningful, and the superficial from the profound.

Finally, a complete understanding of presenting means fully embracing the concept of risk-taking in presenting the performing arts. While the marketplace plays a crucial role, presenters must also strategize for the future—they must think about ideas and art forms that will define our future art and culture. The presenting field includes many individuals with strong beliefs in, and a profound commitment to, art and artists. They readily stake the considerable resources of their organizations on our artistic future, investing in artists who, they believe, have the greatest potential to reshape our culture. I would argue that these investments have rarely been misplaced. A broad range of creative activity must be stimulated within the arts world without regard to its immediate ability to show up as a finished work on a stage somewhere. The energy of a vast array of competing forces, artistic as well as marketplace, can enable creative activity to thrive in this country, and the presenter must be the catalyst to create that energy.

Resources are scarce for artists. Presenters should concern themselves with the fact that work is not being created because resources are not available. What is lost when an artist is unable to develop work in a way that honors the integrity of the artistic process rather than the demands of the marketplace? What happens when we don't allow for full exploration of the creative impulse by gifted artists? Many presenters are personally disheartened and professionally desperate about working in a society that places such a low value on the work of artists. Nonetheless, within the constraints of the system and the resources available, good people do thrive—both presenters and artists— and presenters repeatedly find ways to support, encourage and insure the growth and development of those artists whose work creates our culture. The crucial role that presenters play in this process must be upheld with integrity, passion and a commitment to meeting the challenges of the artistic process.

A presenter takes on enormous responsibilities when agreeing to embark on the practice of presenting. In staking a claim to this role, the profession correspondingly takes on the responsibility to fulfill that role with complete integrity. It is no longer possible for "just anyone" to be a presenter. By recognizing and understanding the full meaning of the practice of presenting, the multiple dimensions of the presenter's work are illuminated and the degree of rigor that we must bring to that work is revealed.

5

UNDERSTANDING THE PRESENTER

Despite the important role they play within the world of art and culture, presenters are often invisible to the communities they serve. Unlike the artist who independently creates distinctly personal work, the presenter is usually the agent of a larger entity or organization. The presenter also works on behalf of the community and therefore has an obligation to the community's trust. That obligation it would seem, mandates expectations and standards of practice. Yet those expectations are rarely, or only superficially, defined and articulated. Characterizing the presenting profession and what it takes for an individual to actually claim the title of presenter then becomes problematic.

Concurrent with a lack of defined expectations and standards of practice has been the presenter's invisibility to the artistic process. The season of events is often presented to the community as if it were designed by no one, or at best, by an unseen hand for reasons not entirely clear. If the presenter had a role in this process, it is often characterized as a commercial one of selecting those events most readily salable to the public. The program is rarely viewed as a carefully curated series of performances specific to this community and designed to fulfill the multiple facets of the presenting role.

Obscuring the role of the presenter is misguided for several reasons. To begin with, it presents art and artists in a contextual vacuum, ascribing universality to the art that neither the artist nor the presenter actually believes in or desires. Failing to articulate the criteria of artistic selection also abbreviates the ongoing critical discourse around art. By remaining invisible, presenters abdicate personal responsibility both for creating the framework for discussion of art and for publicly acknowledging their part in shaping the cultural landscape. In retreating behind a veil of "neutrality," presenters implicitly disavow responsibility for their artistic choices. Without a presenter's defined and articulated context, the dialogue around the work either does not occur or occurs in an unfocused way.

More concretely and equally importantly, failing to acknowledge the full dimension of a presenter's work destabilizes the profession and exacerbates the current situation in which many believe that "anyone can do it." No artist is allowed to perform work anonymously. No presenter should be allowed to work anonymously either. At great risk, the artist puts work before the public and invites discourse and critique. Presenters should do the same.

Consequently, the professional presenter must bring a high degree of rigor to the work. A commitment to designing the performance experience will mean acquiring equal degrees of knowledge, care and concern about the art, the artist and the audience. No one part of this triangle can be neglected or ignored by a successful presenter. Furthermore, the presenter's knowledge and understanding of art, artist and audience is fundamental to his or her professional identity and deserves continual examination and development. Similarly, if the presenter is to be responsible for creating meaning, creating cultural discourse and shaping the culture, then the work demands an extraordinarily high degree of personal intellect, insight into the world and examined ethics. Thus a presenter's work must begin with self-examination.

The Presenter's Relationship to Self

Presenters draw from the same sources as do artists to accomplish their work. Like the artist, the presenter's artistic decision-making springs from experiences, both personal and professional, which have been accumulated throughout a lifetime. Presenters must acknowledge their personal values and beliefs and embrace them as central to the development of a curatorial vision for their work, recognizing that negotiating these values will significantly affect it.

Every presenter approaches the work with a personal aesthetic that has developed through his or her engagement with art. Experiences with art determine not only taste for or against a particular art form, but also the development of a substantive aesthetic rather than a casual list of likes and dislikes.

Presenters should also be cognizant of the need for a continually evolving personal aesthetic. Achieving comprehensive understanding of and appreciation for a particular art form is a laudable and important goal. But presenters should also push beyond their aesthetic comfort zone, particularly those of us engaged in presenting the art of our time. We can see the aesthetic development of an extraordinary artist over the course of his or her lifetime. We should see that same development in presenters.

A personal aesthetic presupposes a critical faculty that allows the presenter to simultaneously appreciate and critique art. Over time, this critique becomes more refined, deeper and better articulated around the nuances of the art. As the presenter's personal aesthetic evolves, the artistic choices made by the presenter reflect this increasing sophistication. The result is that, in this very public role, the presenter leads the development of the community's aesthetic, creating a more informed and more critical audience for the arts. The need to explore further, to pursue deeper, to understand more that drives the artist must also drive the presenter. The presenter shares that pursuit with his or her community through artistic decision-making

Presenting is not, however, a process of simply replicating the presenter's aesthetic for the community, an ultimately self-indulgent exercise. Rather, the presenter mediates between a personal aesthetic and the community circumstances, providing more or less contextualization along the way so that the organizational and community aesthetics can develop organically as the presenter's has. The presenter seeks to provide members of the community with opportunities to develop their own aesthetics. In this way, the presenter's personal aesthetic development drives the presenting experience through translation, not through replication.

Because the presenter's relationship to the community is so key, the presenter's personal relationship to the socio-economic-political environment of the country is also important. Effective presenting requires not only a knowledge and awareness of the environment in which the presenter lives, but also a thoughtful understanding of the presenter's place in that environment.

Arguably the most important aspect of this understanding is recognizing and reckoning with the racial basis upon which this country was created and the racial legacy that the individual presenter brings to the table. It is vital to reflect on and critique one's own role in this history. Each of us must reflect on of how our personal history plays out in our own work.

White men and women, who even today continue to dominate the top jobs in the presenting field, are especially required to examine their inherited privilege and how it has helped them earn their positions. How does their race manifest itself in their work? Are they able to recognize that Eurocentric work is not the universal American aesthetic? Can they envision themselves as participants in undoing the legacy of racism they have inherited? Presenters of color will confront an entirely different and equally complex range of issues around race. Do they aspire to be curator for a larger community than the specifically racialized community in which they might be expected to remain? How can and should they navigate being a racial minority in America? How does this manifest itself in their work? These extraordinary challenges demand a high degree of self-awareness and become a lifelong endeavor for all of us.

Extending this idea to the community, presenters must also recognize the vital role their organizations play in the national discourse about race. Presenters have the unique opportunity to simultaneously provoke dialogue and advance this discourse even as they take active steps to reshape the reality within which the discourse occurs. It's unrealistic to expect that a meaningful discourse about race can grow out of a season that only features the work of Eurocentric artists. An arts ecology that visibly and actively supports and encourages the voices of artists of color with the same passion that it supports other artists can inspire a discourse that can make a difference. Presenters can both participate in the discourse and shape the environment in which it occurs. But like the discourse about aesthetics, it begins with the individual presenter.

A broad range of deeply personal intellectual, psychological and spiritual experiences and beliefs are equally critical to the development of a presenter's self-awareness and will ultimately affect the presenter's work. An individual moral code, a familiarity with or distance from deeply personal psychological questions, a belief in a spiritual being (or not)—dozens of such questions are crucial to the presenter's understanding of a personal identity. The degree of reflection that presenters exercise around self-awareness is as vital to the success of presenting as it is to art-making.

The Presenter's Relationship to Art

Presenters must be passionate about and passionately committed to art, to understanding and exploring it and to insuring that opportunities for artistic production are created. A presenter's relationship to art begins with a personal aesthetic, but it takes on a much larger and more significant role in the presenter's work.

The presenter's personal involvement in art-making often profoundly shapes the understanding and knowledge of art. Fortunately, many presenters enter the field having first been practicing artists themselves. This enables a presenter to have firsthand knowledge of, and respect for, the process of art-making, a respect born of personal experience. Clichés about art-making abound, but those who have done it recognize that it is often messy, frustrating, debilitating hard work, providing moments of great joy and insight and many more of fear, inadequacy, vulnerability and uncertainty.

While some presenters can and do make art, it is often neither practical nor possible for an individual to work simultaneously as an artist and a presenter. Still, presenters must truly understand what occurs in the creative process, must know what it means to be driven by a motivation that cannot be ignored, must understand the need to create or embody an idea completely. Presenters must recognize that frustration and success are both inherent in the creative process, as are impasses and breakthroughs, extraordinary achievement and unanticipated failure. These components can best be understood through experience with art-making. In the process, the specific character of both the art and the artist are revealed to the presenter in ways that will seriously affect his or her work.

Still, presenters must truly understand what occurs in the creative process, must know what it means to be driven by a motivation that cannot be ignored, must understand the need to create or embody an idea completely.

The presenter should also fully understand art from a theoretical perspective and engage in the lifelong process of learning about it. Like art-making, education will produce similar anxieties, frustrations, risks and rewards. The presenter must constantly challenge his or her assumptions and previously held beliefs and understandings about art. More than simply learning about new forms, presenters must reinvestigate familiar forms and reinterpret previous understandings. Committing to a lifelong education about art is intrinsic to the presenter's work.

There are, of course, multiple paths to learning about and understanding art. Attending performances is the primary mode of engaging with art, and there is no substitute for the ongoing, daily practice of experiencing performance. Regardless of the presenter's primary artistic interests and work, encounters with all art forms help develop the presenter's personal aesthetic and critical faculty.

Engagement with the visual arts can be particularly important for a performing arts presenter. Through the visual arts, a presenter can develop a greater visual literacy, understanding performances in visual terms rather than the narrative, text-based and/or linear approaches that often dominate the performing arts. This alternative way of experiencing art can also create opportunities for the presenter to reflect on different approaches to both curating and contextualizing the performance experience for an audience.

Similarly, attending commercial cultural events can enlighten a presenter in understanding audiences and expanding one's sense of what can be accomplished through the performance experience. Popular or commercial culture, because of its access to resources, often explores the boundaries of technology as well as new modes of cultural expression. Since the boundaries between art and commercial culture are so blurred, attention to this aspect is necessary to the presenter's experience with, and education about, the performing arts.

Concurrent with the need to attend performances is the necessity to find or create opportunities to engage in a critical dialogue about art. If there is a singular weakness in the field of presenting, it may be the lack of critical discourse. There are many reasons for this, not the least of which may be the failure on the part of our field to recognize that discussions about art are central to what it means to be a presenter. Many presenters are also insecure about their own critical faculties and conscious of their inability to articulate a thoughtful point of view about art. Unfortunately, the dialogue among presenters about art often rests at the level of "I liked it" or "I didn't like it," a limited discussion of audience reaction and, of course, the degree of financial success.

The engagement of presenters, artists, and audiences in thoughtful dialogue about art is second only to attending performances for the presenter's personal development. Not only should presenters discover what others ("my audience") think about the art, they also need to further develop their own critical faculties. Through such engagement, presenters develop the rigorous personal aesthetic necessary for excellence in the profession.

Presenters can take a leadership role in stimulating dialogue about art within the entire arts community. Too often, that dialogue is left to chance, and bits and pieces occur in response to specific events, creating dialogue that is not sustained and lacks depth. While this supports the generally creative anarchy that is the hallmark of the arts in America, it does little to critically evaluate artistic development and stimulate rigor around creativity and artistic ideas. The mélange of American creativity is robust; it demands similarly robust debate. Presenters can, and should, develop the tools necessary and the opportunities required for a sustained dialogue about art.

Caring for the art has its practical aspects, to be sure, including the presenter's responsibility to create a supportive atmosphere within which great art can be created and flourish. This responsibility encompasses the physical conditions the presenter creates for the artist during performance, but the role also includes using the power and resources available to the presenter to insure that art thrives. This responsibility includes commissioning and producing, which are an increasingly larger part of the presenter's role in the arts ecology. In an era in which direct funding to artists is extremely rare, the need for presenters to sponsor the creation and development of new work has become even more significant. Presenters must fully embrace that responsibility and respond with integrity, generosity and concern for the shaping of the culture.

Attending performances and participating in the cultural dialogue about art are just the beginning of the work the presenter must do. They must also investigate and learn about art and artists as part of their responsibility to lead the development of the arts in our culture. As the steward of the performance experience, presenters must insure that when the interaction between art, artist and audience occurs, it is a significant moment for all involved.

The Presenter's Relationship to the Artist

Understanding the presenter's relationship to the art also requires looking at the presenter's relationship to the artist. Since the growth and development of art fundamentally depends on the growth and the development of the artist, the presenter's relationship to the artist plays a similarly important role in the arts ecology. That relationship should be a multi-dimensional, mutually beneficial partnership. The interaction between artist and presenter is likely to be fluid and dynamic acknowledging the unique contributions that each brings to the artistic endeavor. Most of all, a symbiotic relationship between presenter and artists is significant to the development of the art form. Maintaining equilibrium within the relationship, on both individual and global scales, helps build a healthy arts ecology.

Sometimes, the presenter's relationship to the artist has been characterized as an exploitative aspect of the American system of producing and disseminating the performing arts. This viewpoint idealizes the artist's struggle against a system that provides few immediate or direct financial rewards. But it also demonizes the presenter as the conduit through which resources must travel to reach the artist, with the inevitable "siphoning and censoring" mechanisms which prevent the artist from reaching true creative potential. Understanding and enacting the relationship in this way describes a power dynamic that is not healthy for the artist, the presenter or the field.

A more productive perspective acknowledges the interdependent nature of the relationship of the presenter and the artist. The facts of the partnership remain the same because the artist holds the creative idea and the presenter often holds the mechanics necessary to actualize the artist's idea. An interdependent approach recognizes that neither artist nor presenter can exist without the other and that by working in a true collaboration, both can achieve their individual objectives.

An interdependent approach recognizes that neither artist nor presenter can exist without the other and that by working in a true collaboration, both can achieve their individual objectives.

The presenter's support for the artist and the work can extend from the initial idea, through the creative and incubation process to the performance itself. Even after the "premiere," which for many artists is simply a new starting point for the piece, the presenter's support can be crucial. To do this work effectively, the presenter must thoroughly understand the creative process. Presenters must also understand the conditions under which artists create work to fully appreciate how important his or her role is at different points in the process.

A common challenge to artists is the lack of creative time and the opportunity to allow the creative process to develop organically to its conclusion in new work. From the beginning, the marketplace pressures artists not simply to create but to create successful (often meaning popular) works of art quickly and consistently. Indeed, presenters often pressure artists to "deliver product." Presenters should counter this trend by working with artists to find and produce creative time. Long-term creative residencies, free or minimal cost rehearsal and development space, technological resources and commissioning support are all resources a presenter can offer to support an artist's creative process.

Such actions reflect a presenter's faith and trust in the artist's ability to create great work. This is not about the "opportunity to fail," a phrase that is unworthy and even inaccurate. Artists do not need the opportunity to fail, they need the opportunity to succeed. Thus presenters need to support artists over the long term, even and perhaps especially when the creative impulse leads in directions that may not ultimately end up in a polished, finished product. No scientist is expected to make a "discovery" without first pursuing many experiments that ultimately lead to dead ends. Artists need that same consideration. The crucial role the presenter plays is to insure, through a mutually respectful relationship, that the artistic process is moving towards an end that benefits the artist, the presenter, the art and the audience.

Fulfilling his or her obligations to the artist and the creative process requires that the presenter have extraordinary knowledge of the artists working in the field. Central to the presenter's profession will always be the need to know which artists are active, where they are in their career development, what the artist's particular aesthetic may be and what the artist wishes to pursue within and outside of that aesthetic. Presenters insure the development and support of an art form through the relationships they create and the support they provide to specific artists who are thoroughly engaged in developing the art. Because their resources are limited, presenters must see support for specific artists within the broader context of the art form and respond accordingly. At the same time, focusing on too few artists can produce a narrowing of a single art form or even the place of a specific art form in the context of the entire performance world. The presenter's ability to engage in critical dialogues related to art become ever more important to the work.

Supporting artists throughout the creative process is certainly important. But as a steward of the arts infrastructure in this country, presenters also hold the key to the livelihood of many artists simply by deciding to present (or not) a given artist. Such decisions dramatically affect an artist's career and ability to continue to create. Presenters can provide long-term support for mature artists, nurture younger artists, introduce new artists and support artists who are reinterpreting previously created work.

The need for the presenter to support artists at specific moments in their careers is crucial to the connection between presenter and artist. Certainly the need to nurture young artists is well recognized, but support for the so-called "mid-career" artist is often even harder to find and consequently more critical as the artist develops a mature voice. Similarly, if an artist's career has been temporarily interrupted, support for that artist at a reentry moment can be critical. Again, this is the time for a presenter to be especially responsible in caring for the artist.

Artists within certain genres may often have particular difficulty finding funding. Artists working on the margins of either the art world or our culture often have the most difficulty acquiring support, especially if their work is controversial or addresses issues that, as a culture, we would prefer not to acknowledge. Artists who have achieved success despite poverty, racism and geographic location are especially in need of the presenter's support, inasmuch as they represent the full range of artistic expression in the culture. While artistic Darwinism may allow the strongest and "best" artists to survive, it can also produce a narrow range of artistic expression that is not healthy for the arts or for our culture. Presenters are in a position to subvert these circumstances and they must do so, lest artistic expression become limited to the voices of only those with the most resources.

A presenter who is immersed in the art, who draws on personal experience with the creative process, who cares deeply about artists and creates mutually respectful relationships with them, will be a positive force in support of the art and the artists. It is an enormous responsibility for presenters to decide where to place their limited resources. They must determine which artists to support and decide who has the potential to change the face of our art and culture. Fulfilling that responsibility requires conscientious presenters to make thoughtful and ethical decisions that have profound consequences.

The Presenter's Relationship to the Community

The final important area to consider in relationship to the individual presenter's development rests in his or her relationship to the community. This aspect in particular distinguishes presenting from other artistic endeavors. The research required of a presenter to truly understand the community is no less important than that required for learning about art and artists, and demands an equal degree of rigor. Without a thorough knowledge and understanding of the complexities of one's community, successful presenting is very much at risk.

The community within which presenters work, and indeed for whom they work, affects not only the presenting endeavor but also the organizational identity, the mission and vision and the artistic heart of the organization. Though it is tempting to define the presenting organization in terms of the art it presents, it is more true for the organization to think of itself in terms of the community it serves and the place of the presenting organization within that ecology. An organization may have as its role to introduce new work to the community, to support and affirm community identity through the arts, to provide access to performances otherwise unavailable there, or perhaps to support a specific art form within the community. Inevitably, understanding and articulating the presenter's role in the community creates a focus for presenting and disassociates the presenter from a nondescript "arts for all" rubric.

Presenters need to recognize that their communities are complex, often Balkanized, defiant of easy description, and segmented in multiple, overlapping ways such that any given individual may be part of several sub-communities. Geography is often the first and most practical lens through which the presenter examines and understands the community. It does not take long to recognize the geographical barriers to the movement of people. Occasionally these are physical (rivers, bridges, mountains, well-known traffic bottlenecks), but more often they are sociological and involve intangible barriers that have developed to mark territories and keep people in or out. While the idealistic presenter may think expansively about geography ("everyone within a 50-mile radius is our target market"), such thinking is unrealistic.

Demographics offer another tool for understanding community and sub-communities. Age, race, ethnicity, income, education, standard of living and other demographic data represent the uniform and describable information that agencies collect. This may be the first pass at understanding and describing a community, but it is only the beginning.

While living in Tucson, for example, I learned that the median income there is below the national average. Vast swaths of the city and county were comprised of the working poor or service workers. Conventional wisdom would not place these individuals at the heart of a targeted audience for the arts, so on demographics alone Tucson may initially be viewed as a weak arts community. In fact, demographics revealed only one piece of the picture. Tucson has a vibrant and engaged arts community who, despite their modest income, choose for many reasons to attend arts events in astonishingly high numbers. The key to understanding this lies in understanding their values and their lifestyles.

Psychographics, another way of looking at sub-communities and how they define themselves, examines a person's values and lifestyle choices and groups people according to how they enact those values. Psychographics attempts to understand the "why" of decision-making, an important question for presenters who want to know why people attend performances and why they don't. An entire industry has been constructed around this research, which segments the American market into increasingly finer slices, defining sub- communities in terms of the purchasing decisions that people make. Clearly this is a second wave of understanding which, when overlaid with demographics, begins to create a more nuanced picture of the community.

Even when overlaid on demographic information, however, psychographics still misses key aspects of community life. Presenters must also understand broad social trends that affect community identity. The presenter can, based on partial information, extrapolate the underlying causes of these broad social trends, which are both culturally based and connected to values and lifestyles.

One social trend to analyze is how people create and sustain a life within the community. Much is made of the post-industrial world, the service economy, the creative class and the multiplicity of ways that people create and sustain an economic life. These are not simply questions of income, but of the type of work in which the community engages. Tucson draws people whose values are less related to consumerism and more related to a relaxed, pressure-free quality of life. It actually can be relatively inexpensive to live in Tucson, which is also physically beautiful and has a thriving cultural and artistic scene. Many of the very same service workers with minimal disposable income have great interest in engaging in the arts, and they sustain Tucson's artistic life. Often they are people whose education level might be quite high but who have eschewed the pressures of big-city living in favor of this quieter environment. The same can be said about the retirement community, which, while large, is not the dominant force there. Nor do they fit the generally accepted portrait of inactive retirees.

A second consideration is the community's political composition, which often reflects a range of values important to a successful arts endeavor. While this is usually perceived to be a classically liberal outlook, individuals of a more conservative political point of view may well be deeply interested in supporting the arts. Recognizing that every community has a range of political viewpoints is helpful in developing support for a presenter's artistic vision.

Another aspect of community is spirituality and the role of religious organizations in the lives of the residents. There are marked differences in every community about religious expression and the role of religious institutions in daily life. Even so-called "Bible Belt" communities are not monolithic. In fact, like other social constructs, the religious community within any area is complex and breaks down along multiple strands of thought, influence and certainly power. The complexity of this should not be underestimated. Especially now, presenters would be well served to understand the nuances of the spiritual communities with which they intend to work.

Understanding the social strata of the community is also difficult but equally important. Every community has social hierarchies; the presenter should understand what they are and how to access them. Social hierarchies can be extremely proscriptive in matters related to both demographics and psychographics. Income may be the entry point but beyond that, behavior and activities may be prescribed for continued membership and acceptance in any given social hierarchy. This occurs at all class levels and one of the chief challenges to class aspiration is the fear of leaving a place of familiarity and acceptance for a place where acceptance may not come as easily. Since art is often deeply entwined with class, these are issues of real concern to an arts presenter who intends to diversify the audience for any art form.

For presenters whose organizations purport to serve a broad spectrum of a large community, the relationship with racial and ethnic sub-communities is fundamental to creating a presenting program capable of providing sites for cultural discourse.

Understanding the social strata means investigating and understanding the ways that various communities organize their social lives. The organizations around which people congregate can include schools, churches, synagogues and temples, cultural centers, business-related organizations, social, cultural and recreational organizations and even arts organizations. Looking at the ways a community organizes itself socially tells us much about its values.

For presenters whose organizations purport to serve a broad spectrum of a large community, the relationship with racial and ethnic sub-communities is fundamental to creating a presenting program capable of providing sites for cultural discourse. Historic racism and resource inequities mean marginalized communities will have and support presenters within their own communities who speak to the specific issues of their constituencies. This is a crucial piece of building dialogue in America and requires ongoing support. Only fully realized voices can speak at a larger table with confidence and vitality.

A purported "community-wide dialogue" lacks standing if important voices are omitted from the conversation. Many large institutions, which more often than not represent the majority white culture, make the crucial mistake of presuming to speak for all. Always problematic, this is even more of an issue now with the "browning of America" and the rapid demographic shifts happening in virtually every community. Creating a true cultural dialogue means insuring that all voices are fully and substantially represented in the discourse. It requires that individual strengths be recognized, especially since a true cultural dialogue raises difficult questions of power and resource distribution. For presenters of the dominant culture, developing relationships with historically marginalized or excluded communities requires both boldness and sensitivity. Presenters from marginalized communities face challenges of equity, respect and mutuality of purpose that can create internal as well as external conflict. Irrespective of the challenges, this may be the most important work any presenter can do.

Conclusion

Working as a presenter creates enormous personal and professional challenges for the individual who aspires to success in the profession. It can be daunting work to reflect deeply upon one's own aesthetic and ideas, commit to a lifelong process of learning about art, art-making and artists and engage a community in ways that are difficult and complex. Yet these are the basics of presenting.

The extent to which the presenter researches and develops these basics will largely determine both the integrity and the power of the presenting enterprise. Virtually all presenters grapple with themselves, art, artists and community in some way, and both the organizational philosophy and the presenter's programming reflect how seriously the presenter takes on the challenge. For some, understanding the art means annual trips to the booking conferences and conversations with a few trusted managements. Some presenters think little about the long-term support of artists, considering only the immediate needs of the upcoming presenting season. Worse, presenters may treat artists as commodities and subject the artist and the field to the "flavor of the month" phenomenon, simply picking up on what seems hot at the moment and seeking success through imitation. Some presenters limit their understanding of the community to their own circle of friends, their boards, their advisory committees—to whomever purports to speak on behalf of the larger group. Others take audience opinion surveys to give them what they want so as not to have to do the hard work of really understanding the complexity of the community. Gross generalizations are drawn about entire communities based on the uninformed opinions of a few. Presenters may carelessly throw out the phrase "my community is not ready for it" when what they really mean is that they themselves are unfamiliar with or unmoved by an artist or art form. Such a position is a clear indication of the presenter's need to do more work and achieve a deeper understanding of the art and the challenges it presents.

These approaches to presenting, while common, do disservice to the field, to the artists and to our communities. The nature of the performance experience and its resonance cannot be denied. The enormous power of the presenter to affect lives demands a passionate, lifelong commitment to learning and an unceasing quest for more information, greater understandings and an evolving sense of consciousness about art and the world.

In asserting this point of view, I do not devalue the administrative and managerial aspects of presenting work. The ability to function skillfully in the marketplace is essential to successful presenting. The presenter generally works for a mission driven, non-profit organization, but invariably connects daily with the marketplace to affect the vision of the organization. The ability to negotiate contracts is as important to a presenter's success as his or her understanding of self, art, artists and community.

But engaging this work with integrity — being a presenter — requires more than a good grasp of the balance sheet, an ability to negotiate effectively and the marketing and fundraising knowledge to support the endeavor. While these skills support the presenter's work, the creation of the performance experience, the shaping of culture and the creation of cultural discourse are the real work and, indeed, the real challenge of presenting.

◆6◆

THE ORGANIZATIONAL FRAMEWORK FOR PRESENTING

Organizational structure and curatorial vision comprise the paradigm within which presenters do their work. The concept of a nonprofit performing arts presenter is well established and, with its meaning centered in mission, vision and values, is most appropriate for the presenting endeavor. Before moving on to a discussion of curatorial vision and practice, however, it's worth re-examining these core concepts as well as a fourth, aesthetic core, that is equally crucial to the organizational framework for presenting.

Nonprofit arts organizations are guided by their mission statements. Often driven by external forces (funders, parent organizations, marketers, governments), organizations have been known to struggle to create a mission statement that will be the driving force of their organization. In far too many cases, they end up with "McMission" statements—statements of purpose so general that they could apply to dozens of similar organizations. Often focused around presenting "high quality, diverse artists," these aphorisms do little to address the fundamental issues of organizational purpose. Despite the title of "mission" statement, they do even less to motivate or guide the actions of the organization.

A simple one-sentence statement of "what we do" cannot adequately articulate the philosophical basis from which a presenting organization exists, nor can it serve as a comprehensive description of organizational principles and aspirations. Instead, presenters and boards need to grapple with and ultimately articulate the organization's mission, vision, and values to establish the essential nature of the organization. Each of these statements has a limited focus that articulates, fully and thoughtfully, different but important aspects of organizational identity. Together, they provide the philosophical foundation that creates and sustains the organization and serves as the platform from which the presenting endeavor emanates.

A mission statement is simply a statement of organizational purpose. In the most succinct terms possible, it identifies what the organization is, what it does, for whom and why. It articulates the specific purpose of the organization, the needs it addresses and the real or potential recipients of the organization's work. While it answers some key questions of purpose, it is not fully descriptive of the organization and its artistic program.

The vision statement articulates the organizational aspirations. In the vision statement, the organization sets forth a compelling conceptual image of the future of the organization, an ideal, a vision for the future. The vision should be inspirational, challenging and idealistic. More than the mission statement, it represents the dreams of the organization and implies a pathway to achieving that vision. It provides an opportunity to articulate the organization's role within the community and the world with integrity and enthusiasm.

Many organizations struggle with the aspirational quality of the vision statement, as do those presenters who are most practical in their attitudes. Concrete thinkers are often skeptical about vision statements that articulate an organization or a world that is vastly different than the current one, especially when such aspirations seem impossible to achieve at the moment. Yet the vision statement, even more than the mission statement, defines the organization's purpose. Without a compelling vision, the difficult and demanding work of the presenting organization lacks both direction and meaning.

Together with the mission statement and the vision statement, the values statement completes the organizational identity. The values statement of the organization articulates the core beliefs and philosophies of the organization. A values statement does not describe what the organization will do, but instead articulates the parameters within which actions will occur and the shared beliefs that will guide the decision-making process. In many ways, a values statement sets limits.

To these essential three components, I would add a fourth which, while rarely discussed, is nonetheless a vital part of organizational identity. The aesthetic core, the overriding conceptualization of the artistic heart of the organization, is a description of identity that is often missing from the organization's articulated sense of itself. Perhaps this is because the artistic heart is obvious to the board and staff, but it's just as likely that they have simply not spent much time considering the idea. The aesthetic core is a significant component of organizational definition because it sets out clearly the artistic context within which the organization will work. Without an aesthetic core, a presenting organization may be defined by a laudable but too narrowly focused goal of selling tickets and achieving a balanced budget. The aesthetic core, and its actualization through an artistic vision and curatorial practice, defines the presenting organization.

The Aesthetic Core

In 1990, Nello McDaniel and George Thorn published a book titled *The Workpapers One: Rethinking and Restructuring the Arts Organization.* The book provides recommendations and case studies for arts organizations for coping with changing realities. Fundamental to what they recommend is a rethinking of what McDaniel and Thorn refer to as the organization's "aesthetic core." While they were writing primarily for arts-producing organizations, the concept is, I believe, valid for presenters and equally important to their organizational identity. McDaniel and Thorn define the aesthetic core as "...the artistic point of view, the vehicle by which an arts organization realizes its philosophy. The aesthetic core is not the choice of plays, dance or music to be performed. It is the context in which these choices are made."[3] This concept articulates a fundamental need for an artistic point of view for the presenter's work. It requires that an organization see itself first and foremost as an arts organization.

The presenting field has often resisted the idea of presenters as something other than facilitators of the work of artists. Consequently, presenters have often been dismissed by those who view them as "sponsors," "organizers," "contract negotiators" or "venue owners" with a limited understanding of, or vision around, art. To some degree, many presenters have supported this point of view because they too have understood their work as administrative rather than creative. That point of view has not only diminished the field within the context of the arts world but more importantly, it has lowered the expectations presenters have of themselves and their work. By recognizing that the work of the presenter is, in fact, anchored in artistic decision-making—an aesthetic core—the nature of the field is redefined in an important way.

The aesthetic core is simultaneously restrictive and liberating since, as McDaniel and Thorn indicate, it is about context, the aesthetic framework in

[3] Nello McDaniel and George Thorn, *The Workpapers One; Rethinking and Restructuring the Arts Organization* (New York: FEDAPT, 1990), p. 51.

which curatorial decisions are subsequently made, not the specific decisions themselves. One presenting organization might have as its aesthetic core the presentation and support of "contemporary dance by living choreographers." Another might be "the great works of western European art music by composers of the 17th through 19th centuries" or "the full range of American jazz music and musicians of the 20th century." While these are shorthand descriptions that demand more fully developed explanations, they at least indicate the artistic heart of the organizational aesthetic. And they establish the basis from which curatorial decisions are made.

For multidisciplinary presenting organizations, articulating an aesthetic core can be more complicated, but even more important, since it establishes some boundaries to the organization's artistic heart. Without it, the organization can easily drift in many artistic directions, some of which will pull the organization well away from its core artistic mission toward a marketplace focus. As the pressures to earn income through ticket sales increase, multidisciplinary presenters are particularly susceptible to being pushed in the direction of profitable performances based on "what sells" rather than any kind of artistic criteria. Lack of an aesthetic core can mean loss of organizational purpose in ways that are truly devastating for the organization and the community.

Since so many presenting organizations, large and small, are multidisciplinary, the very concept of such an organizational choice bears examination. First, why have the organization's creators chosen to make it multi-disciplinary? The answer to this question is often historical ("we always have been"), structural ("our institution requires it") or situational ("no one else in our community is presenting this work"). But examining the organization's history may well show that it began as a single discipline organization and then expanded over time. What started as a jazz series grew to include other types of music; what began as a dance season eventually embraced theater and popular entertainment. In and of themselves, these may not be misguided aesthetic evolutions, so long as they were conscious and reflective of determined organizational development. The first step in articulating an aesthetic core for multi-disciplinary organizations should be to revisit the idea of multidisciplinarity itself.

Structural and situational mandates about multidisciplinary programming also should be examined before they are accepted and actualized. Many may find that their organizations are multidisciplinary for reasons that have little to do with the interconnectedness of the arts. Multidisciplinary programming may have arisen from a desire to serve multiple audiences and multiple community needs. Working with scarce resources, these organizations may have evolved into programs that present many art forms but none thoroughly enough to create a real impact. The de facto aesthetic core may be focused at "the broadest possible audience," which often translates into an amorphous middle ground both in art and audience. The result is a program that aspires to serve everyone and ultimately serves no one well. In its attempt to be artistically diverse, the program can become superficial and the presenter's impact in the community similarly diluted.

A different way to think about multidisciplinary programming is to conceptualize the aesthetic core from an interrelated perspective based on the core tenets of presenting rather than the more common genre representation perspective. In this construct, the vision of the presenting organization is a site for creating meaning and cultural discourse through a curated series of performances irrespective of artistic genre. For presenters of limited means and without access to an encyclopedic range of artists, this may also be the most practical way to proceed.

The dilemma of disciplinary thinking on any level is that the arts world is increasingly blurring, bending and breaking the walls that have separated disciplines. More artists are refusing to be pigeonholed into a single discipline and do not want their work to be similarly characterized. Furthermore, the discussion around the discipline question ("Is that really dance?") is academic at best, irrelevant at worst. Multi-disciplinary presenters can join with artists in breaking these boundaries and increase interest in and appreciation for many forms of work. Furthermore, the presenter can shift the audience focus away from genre and towards the idea of the artist's work in ways that can be profound for art, artist and community.

As with the mission, vision and values, affirming the aesthetic core is a significant organizational decision for its trustees. The individual presenter, however, is responsible for creating the program, making the specific artistic choices that will illuminate the aesthetic core. Thus, the presenter's personal aesthetic becomes entwined with the organizational aesthetic. Both the board and the presenter need to acknowledge this important intermingling of the personal and the organizational around the artistry of the organization. In the end, the strength of the presenter's personal aesthetic and its coherence with the aesthetic core of the organization will be key to its success.

This being the case, trustees need to exercise both care and courage in selecting the presenter who will make the artistic decisions on behalf of the organization. A presenter cannot work toward the organizational vision without committing unequivocally to the organization's aesthetic core. Presenting organizations have failed when, in their search for a great presenter, a board or administrator has focused on administrative skill first and only tangentially on the candidate's aesthetic sensibilities. Difficult as it may be for the hiring body to approach this discussion and make an informed decision, it is vital that the presenter's personal aesthetic be understood, appreciated and completely coherent with the aesthetic core.

For the presenter, the organization's aesthetic core is an important tool in establishing and maintaining the necessary distance from and connection to the art. The ability to negotiate personal passion, organizational aesthetic and economic realities will determine the presenter's success or failure and the success or failure of the organization.

The aesthetic core is the crucial fourth leg of the organization's identity. Together with the mission, vision and values, the aesthetic core completes a quadrangle of ideas that establish the conceptual basis from which the organization pursues its work. The four statements are dynamic and interactive. With them in place, the director and board establish the philosophical foundation from which the organization operates.

◆7◆

THE PRESENTER'S CURATORIAL PROCESS

A FEW YEARS AGO, I VISITED AN ART MUSEUM RENOWNED FOR ITS COLLECTION OF NATIVE American art. Shortly after entering the museum, I was completely overwhelmed. The museum does in fact have a huge collection of southwestern Indian art and it seemed as if all of it was on display. Even as someone who was somewhat familiar with the work, I found it all to be too vast and uncontextualized to be a particularly effective arts experience. Though the collection was organized by chronology and form, there was little else available to help visitors navigate it. In less than an hour, everything seemed to blend together and I was no longer interested in trying to engage with the art.

Several weeks later, I was in Washington, D.C., and went to the Sackler Gallery of Asian Art to see an exhibition titled *Devi: The Great Goddess*. This was an exhibition of paintings, drawings, and sculpture created from ancient to contemporary times, all related to the Hindu goddess Devi. The curator had carefully selected a relatively small number of objects for this exhibition. But the story those objects told about the goddess and her place in the pantheon of Hindu deities and her relationship to the gods was brilliantly illustrated by this carefully selected group of objects. Organized by idea rather than chronology or genre, the exhibition was designed both to highlight the unique qualities of each object and to tell the larger story. How much more engaging and inspiring this was for a visitor like myself than the plethora of objects that I had found at the other museum! The exhibit raised questions, stimulated thought and provoked unexpected intellectual and aesthetic encounters.

The contrast of these two experiences illustrates the power of a curator to shape an artistic experience, to tell a story with the art. It also illustrates the importance of a considered curatorial practice to the successful presentation of the art. That power and that importance are inherent in the work of the performing arts presenter as well.

For several years now, the presenting field has grappled with this concept of the presenter as curator. Many in the field reject the label as too limited a description of the presenter's work. Others find it pretentious and, celebrating the "practical" roots of the presenting profession, avoid what they consider to be affected language. Others react negatively to the idea that the work of the presenter equates to the work of a museum curator, the profession for which the term has its most widely accepted usage.[4]

Devo-Great Goddess/Freer Gallery of Art*

The word "curator" derives from the Latin, *curare*, which means "to take care of." A search of various web based dictionaries yields a range of definitions that don't veer far from the Oxford English Dictionary's concise "a keeper of a museum or other collection" and include such phrases as "administrative director", "overseer" "in charge of," "manager," "organizer" and the like. Curator is most often used in reference to collections of objects—historical, artistic, scientific—and therefore may seem alien to the idea of the performing arts which concerns itself not with objects but with artists. Can one "curate" artists? Or more precisely for the performing arts, can one curate the performance experience? I believe the answer is yes.[5]

---

[4] Even in the museum world, and especially in contemporary visual arts, the definition and the role of the curator is hotly debated, with varying opinions now offered of what constitutes the work of the curator. See *Curating in the 21st Century*, edited by Gavin Wade and other sources listed in the bibliography for a few examples of books that explore the contours of this debate in the Visual Arts. In researching for this book, I turned often to the visual arts world for context and insights about curating.

[5] Interestingly, some contemporary artists have begun to resist the fetishizing of the object in what they view as the highly commodified world of visual arts. Their art "object" has become, not a physical thing but instead is an "experience" And they define the interaction between artist and audience as the object. Make bread with an artist; eat dinner and talk with the artist; take class with the artist. These are "curated" experiences and curators follow suit with "exhibitions" of "experiences" that are "time-based art" with no physical object to be displayed, bought or sold.

* Painting: Goddess Bhadrakali Worshiped by the Gods: from a tantric Devi series; South Asian, ca. 1660-1670 Opaque watercolor, gold, silver and beetle; wing cases on paper 21.7 x 21.5 cm (8 9/16 x 8 7/16 in.); Origin: Basohli, India; Historical Region: Basohli; Freer Gallery of Art, Smithsonian Institution, Washington, D.C., Purchase, F1984.42

Despite the limited definitions of the dictionaries, curating as a practice is generally understood to be a multifaceted endeavor that certainly involves caring for the objects but also encompasses practices of interpretation, documentation, and making the art accessible to the public. In today's world it has also come to encompass a host of administrative functions including raising the money to make the exhibitions possible. I would argue that these actions by a curator are analogous to, if not definitive of, the work of the presenter. Certainly presenters care for the artists and the development of the artist's work. In addition to commissioning and nurturing new work, presenters insure that the artist's work has a life through the vital endeavor of touring. Unquestionably, in the last several years in particular, presenters have become highly invested in issues of interpretation, making art accessible to audiences and, to a somewhat lesser degree, documentation. And no presenter would deny that finding the funding to support the creation and touring of performing arts consumes a substantial amount of his or her time and energy.

Recognizing these similarities, the term "curator" in relation to the work of the presenter has recently become more widespread in its usage. Understanding our role as curators, and acknowledging the vital importance of the curatorial process, has also benefited the field of presenting and the performing arts in general. In addition to accurately describing the presenter's work it carries with it an expectation of rigor, especially around artistic choices, that has been missing in the presenting field. Demanding of presenters that they bring the same degree of research, thought and care to their work as a curator does, helps to insure that the presenting endeavor achieves the impact of which it is capable.

The curatorial process is the most important aspect of the presenter's work. It represents the actualization of the organization's mission, vision, values and aesthetic core. It is the primary marker of organizational identity, the vehicle by which the public understands the organization and assesses its value to the individual and the community. The curatorial process determines which performances are offered to the public and establishes the performance as the site of cultural discourse within the community.

It is also the aspect of presenting that is, by and large, the least well understood or discussed within the profession. Most presenters receive little or no training or education in curating and willingly confess that, in the crush of business, thinking about "programming" consumes a small percentage of their time, even though a question often asked of the presenter is, "How (or why) did you select these artists for this season?" Indeed, audiences, critics, funders and others engaged in commentary about arts presenting often critique presenters based on their curatorial work.

Four interdependent parts comprise the practice of curating the performing arts—the curatorial idea, the discovery and selection of work, the contextualization of the performance, and the performance itself. Each of these parts of the process gain their power from their interdependency. Though they appear to be linear and sequential, as a complete process they generally are not nor should they be. If the process assumes an organic path, ideas and actions from one area feed into other areas, creating a more integrated curatorial endeavor. This approach also allows for a spiraling of curatorial projects (usually recognized as the presenter's season of work) over time so that insights initially revealed in one season move to centrality in a second season, which then develop further in a similarly organic manner. In this way, not only is there meaningful coherence from season to season, there is also organic growth and development of a long-term curatorial vision.

The Curatorial Idea

The curatorial idea provides the rationale for the construction of the curated project or series. A series that has been curated, as opposed to merely assembled, should have an idea behind it that provides not only an organizing principle for the curator, but also an interpretive focus for the audience.

The curatorial idea may be expressed in a title and conceived and articulated in many ways. It also suggests intentionality, a recognition that these events were brought together deliberately and not randomly or as an accident of scheduling. Thus the idea itself begins the contextualization process for the audience.

The *Devi* exhibit at the Sackler Gallery illustrated well the importance of the idea. It was clear that exploring the concept of "goddess" was the motivation behind the exhibition. The idea had obviously guided the curator in selecting the objects for the exhibit. It certainly provided an interpretive framework for the viewer. The museum of Native American art, on the other hand, did what an unfortunately large number of presenters do, providing arguably great art with no real interpretive framework. The result was a substantially different experience and much less effective for the audience.

Discovery and Selection of Work

The second component of the curatorial process, the discovery and selection of work, is far more complex than simply contacting an artist or agent to see if the artist is available and will fit into a slot of the season being planned. It begins with the presenter's research about the art form, and extends to finding and understanding the work of artists, their history, their current practices and their future developments. What are artists working on? How are they transforming the art form? How can the work connect with and illuminate the curatorial idea? Establishing artist availability comes at the end, not the beginning, of this process.

Contextualization

Contextualization of the performance includes all of the ideas, programs, communications and projects necessary to successfully create the dynamic connection between artist, art and audience. It certainly includes such decisions as finding the proper performance space, choosing the most appropriate dates for the performance, acquiring the necessary funds and all of the other myriad conceptual and logistical details that are the substance of the presenter's work. It also extends to all the plans and activities that presenters generally refer to as "education" or "audience development" which help to establish the interpretive framework within which the presenter enables the audience to understand the artist's work. In creating context, the presenter creates an environment that insures a deeper and more thoughtful engagement with the art.

The Performance

The performance represents both the end and the beginning of the presenter's work in the curatorial process model. While presenters are certainly concerned with the transformational impact of the performance experience when it occurs, arguably the end of the process, they are also concerned with the future directions revealed through it. What curatorial ideas are stimulated by the performance? What contextualization can or must be undertaken as a next step? What other artists will be most appropriate for this community and this organization's vision? By viewing the performance this way, presenters insure that the curatorial vision for the organization develops organically over time.

Many presenters will readily acknowledge that they spend most of their time on logistical issues and not nearly as much as they would like on conceiving the idea or discovering the work. Preparing for and presenting the performance are relatively concrete activities for which one can readily design strategies and see results. Conceiving the idea and discovering the artists that illuminate the idea are more elusive challenges that often do not occur on the schedule that drives the presenter's work. This part of our work is less linear and more fraught with complications and surprises, less amenable to the presenter's highly developed problem-solving skills. Nonetheless, these activities deserve the primary focus of the presenter's attention.

By thinking about the curatorial process through the lens of these four basic but interrelated components, a more complete definition of performing arts presenting emerges, one that more fully articulates the multiple dimensions of that work. If we understand the curatorial process as one of a presenter actively engaging art and audiences within an interpretive framework through a curated season of performances while preparing a context for the work to be received by the audience, a more dynamic paradigm of performing arts presenting results that offers greater opportunities for transformation and impact.

Actively engaging audiences within an interpretive framework connects directly to the idea of seeing the performance experience as the essence of the presenter's work and deepens the way that presenters generally think about curating. The presenter's thinking now begins with the audience and the idea, not simply the artist. Rather than asking, "What artists do I want to present?", the question becomes, "What ideas are arising out of this artist's work and to what extent are they meaningful to my community now?" The audience's experience becomes central to the presenting endeavor.

This approach demands that the presenter think seriously about audiences and the creation of meaning within the arts experience. It also means thinking deeply about who is in the audience and, just as importantly, who is not? Given the vision of the organization, how does the context for the performance need to change, diversify, expand or contract to effectively address the desired audience?

Engaging actively in audience and interpretation also means thinking more rigorously about the art, beginning with the content of the work and then extending to the curatorial idea that drives the series of performances. It demands that the presenter consider performances in relationship to each other as much as their singularity. Within this framework, the presenter creates possibilities for the audience to more deeply engage in interpretive activity around the performance itself, the relationship of the performances and the curatorial idea. In this way, the performance experience becomes both a site for the creation of meaning and a site of public discourse.

Addressing the concept of actively engaging audiences within an interpretive framework ultimately leads the presenter back to the "why" question that drives the curatorial process – the curatorial idea. Thinking about the curatorial idea provokes the question "Why this idea at this particular moment?" Knowing what questions truly need to be asked at a particular moment is a further rationale for the presenter's engagement in the world of ideas.

Engaging actively in audience and interpretation also means thinking more rigorously about the art...

The emergence of the curatorial idea is often more intuitive than it is analytic. The presenter, through his or her research, sees what artists are doing and what ideas in the contemporary world they find compelling and around which they are creating work. Similarly, community research and engagement in the world provides the presenter with his or her own assessment of the important issues and ideas confronting a contemporary world. It is the melding of these two visions into a curatorial idea that underlies the work of the presenter and creates, one hopes, an important season of performing arts.

The need to fully embrace and expand on the interpretive framework further emphasizes the importance of the contextualization process. An enormous range of activities can follow that include but go well beyond advertising the performance and preparing the performance space. In the past several years, the presenting community has increasingly turned its attention to this aspect of the presenting task and contextualization activities have become routine. Many artists and presenters now recognize that these once ancillary activities are in fact central to the presenting endeavor and critical to the audience's experience.

An expansive view of contextualization, however, goes well beyond pre-concert lectures and post-concert talks. If the presenter begins from the assumption that there is no shared background, language or experience around the art, then both the magnitude of the task as well as the opportunities to address it increase dramatically. Many barriers—intellectual, emotional, social and cultural—stand between the audience and the art. From the smallest details of logistics to the most elaborate projects of symposia, panels, lectures, printed materials, artist encounters, participatory activities and any number of the vast array of contextual activities possible, the presenter can, and should, work to deconstruct the barriers and create pathways of understanding between art and audience.

I would add that challenging the ideas of the center (the so-called mainstream) and the periphery is an additional curatorial objective. Feminism, queer theory, post-colonial theory and the politics of representation have deconstructed and reconstituted contemporary thinking about what is the center and what is the periphery. Presenters are uniquely positioned to illuminate this change with a thoughtful and provocative program that views the contemporary world through a lens other than that of the dominant culture.

The 2000 census further justifies this altered view of the world. The picture of the United States that emerges from the demographic data and the corresponding projection into the future shows a rapidly changing sociological reconfiguration in terms not only of race, age and gender, but also of living patterns, domestic habits, and by extension, the goals and aspirations of people who were never part of the dominant culture, nor even aspired to it. For presenters, this eliminates any hesitation about the need to dramatically diversify their programming in every way. Presenters are uniquely positioned to advance a dialogue that is already occurring, bring the arts firmly into that dialogue and extend it in ways that can be intellectually and sociologically profound for audiences and communities. This is an opportunity and a responsibility not to be missed.

Thinking in this admittedly complex way about the presenter's curatorial process illustrates the enhanced importance of the presenter's work. Deeply engaged in issues of art, artists, audience, community and world, the presenter assumes a vastly more important role than that of a "booker" or "sponsor" of performances. Similarly, the work takes on a greater degree of importance than simply creating entertaining experiences for audiences.

•8•

CURATORIAL ROLES

Understanding the curatorial process is the basis for the beginning of the presenter's work. Differences in presenters' organizations and communities means that the nature of the curatorial activity in which he or she engages will differ. Within the curatorial process itself, the presenter will assume particular curatorial roles and implement specific curatorial strategies to actualize the over-arching vision of the organization.

Like the curatorial process, curatorial roles and strategies are not simple matters. Over time, even within a single organization, the presenter will assume various curatorial roles and strategies. Thus it is important for the presenter to have a broad understanding of the possibilities in both areas and be able to move easily between them, adopting the appropriate roles and strategies as circumstances dictate.

Many presenters understand their curatorial role as that of organizer, the person who arranges the performances so they are made accessible to the audience. Logistics and ease of access drive this idea and, in fact the role of organizer is at least part of the presenter's role as curator, no matter how it is defined. But it barely begins to explore the potential of the presenter as curator and how performances and audiences can be brought together within an interpretive framework.

Expanding on the concept of organizer, a presenter may approach the curatorial process as a mapmaker, drawing the outlines, the boundaries, the roads and the topography of the landscape that will guide the audience member to the work. As an organizer, the presenter simply selects events and orders them in some coherent, often linear, fashion. As a mapmaker, the presenter helps the audience navigate through the selected events. That navigation can follow many routes—artistic, chronological, geographic. A curated series of string quartets, for example, might provide comparisons in structure and form that map out the terrain of the string quartet repertoire. The same series of work could be presented chronologically, but the depth of the work might be more effectively mapped if performances and repertoire are positioned for their comparative structures. Generally, this approach presupposes the audience's knowledge and understanding of the art form.

Another potential curatorial role is that of educator, in which the presenter assumes two primary functions. First, the presenter introduces the audience to work with which they may not be familiar. It might be completely new or unknown work, or it could be new developments of work with which the audience has some knowledge. Exploring the full range of the jazz form could, for example, mean introducing Ornette Coleman to an audience which has known primarily Duke Ellington. Second, the presenter provides the context for this new knowledge so the audience can assimilate it. While the contextualization function is clearly key to the curatorial process, when the presenter serves as educator, contextualization takes a primary place.

The presenter can also act as storyteller, linking performances to one another to create a narrative. The narrative in its entirety is more interesting than a single idea and creates a relevant and important chronicle. The stories might be as simple as the history of jazz or as complex as the sociological development of Jews in America as seen through the development of music and dance. The storytelling may be deliberately ahistorical in order to tell a more complex story not reflected simply by the chronology. In every case, the intention is to create a narrative.

Some presenters may see their curatorial role as essayist. In this capacity, the presenter curates a season that puts forward a central question or idea. The intent is to select performances around the idea and argue a particular point of view. In an essay, a thesis is articulated; performances illustrate that thesis and the audience understands and engages in the argument. For example, a presenter might create a series that argues that, in fact, Salieri's music, even though ultimately eclipsed by Mozart's, is equally as profound. Works are carefully selected, activities are designed and the thesis is illustrated through the performances.

The presenter may decide to take on the role of explorer, providing opportunities for the audience to delve into artists or ideas previously unknown. Rather than proposing a thesis as the essayist might, the presenter creates a series of performances that offer the possibility for discovery and new understandings by the audience. In this role, the presenter may not articulate or even imply a thesis but instead foregrounds questions. This approach demands more work from the audience, requiring that they pursue ideas or directions that might never have occurred to them. It is deliberately challenging and creates opportunities for the audience to use their own imaginative resources. If a presenter is interested in presenting a series of contemporary dance performances, for example, it can be curated such that it explores multiple approaches to contemporary dance aesthetics.

In the role of creator of dialogue, the presenter deliberately creates opportunities for dialogue, even controversy. The nature of that dialogue may be internal, within the individual, or external, among the audience and community. The curated series encourages the audience to rethink its preconceived ideas and engages the artist in a dialogue about those ideas. The art deliberately positions alternative points of view, testing widely held notions with countervailing ideas, and stimulating dialogue.

The provocateur combines the internal process of change with the external process of action, propelling an individual and/or a community into self-recognition and the subsequent pursuit of a moral or social action.

Finally, there is the presenter as provocateur, a role in which the presenter deliberately provokes the individual, the audience and/or the community and which extends the curatorial role. The provocateur combines the internal process of change with the external process of action, propelling an individual and/or a community into self-recognition and the subsequent pursuit of a moral or social action. By provoking the individual and the community, presenters create life-changing performances that energize people about their existence, their place in the world and their ability and desire to move forward. Simultaneously, the presenter will work within and outside the organization to carry through the ideas sparked by the project. As provocateur, the presenter insures that art is seen and understood by the community as a force for social and cultural change and that self-awareness, communal understanding and moral and ethical development are intrinsic to the role of the arts in society.

A presenter rarely occupies any one of these roles exclusively. More likely, a presenter will establish an amalgamated identity that emphasizes different roles at different times, dependent on circumstances. At Yerba Buena Center for the

Arts, a contemporary arts center, I certainly see our curatorial role encompassing nearly all of these roles at one time or another, even though our overarching role is probably that of explorer, creator of dialogue and even provocateur.

The presenter's curatorial role may evolve over time as the organization's artistic identity is established, audiences are developed and the community changes. Indeed, it is grasping this changing role that can be most difficult for many presenters who have been in their positions for a long time and are unable or unwilling to move out of the "organizer" role into a new one.

Regardless of the role assumed, presenters should be both conscious of their roles and attentive to the demands and expectations such an assumption places on their work. By taking on curatorial roles, the presenter structures a curatorial framework for the performance series, sets an interpretive framework for making important connections between art, artist and audience and works toward achieving the total vision of the organization.

◆9◆

CURATORIAL STRATEGIES

A CURATORIAL ROLE ESTABLISHES A POINT OF VIEW, A FRAMEWORK WITHIN WHICH THE presenter then uses curatorial strategies to achieve the goals of the organization. Through these curatorial strategies, the presenter actualizes the curatorial role, bringing to life the ideas that guide the selection of work and the creation of contextual activities that accompany the performances and the entire series.

Like curatorial roles, the curatorial strategies that a presenter pursues will also change according to what the presenter is seeking to accomplish at any given time. Experience with the practice of presenting and engaging in the curatorial process will help presenters discover new strategies that work for their organization at any given time.

I think about these strategies in two broad categories: those driven by thinking primarily about the art, and those driven by thinking primarily about the audience. Since the process is fluid and dynamic, however, these strategies should be viewed as areas of emphasis and direction and not as rigid boundaries.

To begin with, however, I want to address the concept of "excellence" in the performing arts. Presenters' most common, and correspondingly most problematic, approach to their work is the stated pursuit and presentation of "excellence," or "high quality" art as a curatorial strategy. While this is often used to define the organization's aesthetic core, and is equally unhelpful there, its use as a curatorial strategy indicates a misunderstanding of the role of the presenter as curator. For a presenter to stake a claim to excellence is either to state the obvious (no presenter embraces "mediocrity" as a curatorial strategy) or to create a sufficiently broad statement into which virtually anything can fall. (Remember the southwestern art museum and its proliferation of excellent art!) It also initiates a circular discussion about excellence that generally leads nowhere. "It was good" becomes the end point of the consideration of the art.

But we cannot, nor should we, either avoid or eliminate the discussion of excellence as it applies to art. The concept more appropriately belongs as an organizational value, underpinning all the presenter's work. A presenter strives for excellence in financial management, in marketing strategies, in the personnel hired and in the art that is presented. Excellence is the place from which the curatorial strategy begins, rather than ends.

Thinking about the Art

The most common curatorial strategy in the presenting world is probably curating by genre; the presenter defines the series, the season and often the organization itself by a specific artistic genre. It may be as generic as music, theater or dance, or it may be more narrowly focused to jazz, modern dance, ballet, or chamber music. Interestingly, while presenters gravitate to this curatorial strategy, many artists resist being pigeonholed around a specific artistic genre, desiring to be recognized by the artistic range of what they do rather than a convenient artistic label.

The strength in a genre approach is that it uses terminology and a shorthand that usually communicates clearly and specifically to the intended audience what they will experience. Potential audiences may have little or no knowledge of the specific work of the artists on the season, so this categorization may help them decide whether or not they are likely to enjoy or even recognize the specified events. But this approach is also relatively unimaginative and uninteresting. It does little to focus a potential audience outside of their preconceived ideas of what interests them. If an individual loves dance, he or she knows which organization presents dance or which series within an organization is the dance series. The reverse is true as well; the individual who dislikes classical music skips over series or events that might be quite interesting and accessible because they carry the negative code of the genre name.

The genre approach also strengthens boundaries that are actually becoming more fluid. What is "dance-theater," anyway?" Does it matter? Which series does it belong to, dance or theater? Who gets to decide—curator, artist or audience? Genre curating also sets up increasingly immutable audience expectations. The audience reaction to placing an event on a dance series that may not be considered dance by the audience, but is by the artists and/or curator, establishes a negative framework from the outset and creates a situation in which the audience can feel duped into attending an event that is not what it claimed to be.

Because of its generic quality and because of the deficient cultural discourse about art in this country, genre presenting calcifies artistic genres and normalizes a specific type of art. This makes the margins of art even more unacceptable to a larger audience. A steady diet of western European art music on a music series suggests that this music is the mainstream and places all other music outside that mainstream. While western European art music can certainly stake a claim to being profound, highly developed and broad and deep in its impact, so can many other types of music. Yet the rest of this music is usually described as something else, often as "world" music, as if there is western European art music and then the rest of the world's music. This is neither appropriate nor healthy for music in general.

Similarly, marginalization and ghettoization can occur when performances by artists of color are separated into their own genre. In delineating "black dance," "Latino music," or "Asian theater," an intent to highlight or honor an art form can end up setting it apart, which is ultimately detrimental to the artist and the art form. Fortunately, this curating by identity politics can be subverted by situating work by artists of color in a different context. In so doing, the presenter honors the culture of the artist while simultaneously placing the art into, rather than outside, the so-called mainstream.

Another common curatorial strategy related to art is stylistic. Like the genre strategy, this approach is often seen in organizational identity and aesthetic core as much as it is in a curatorial vision. Thus there are "world music" presenters, "contemporary performance" presenters, "classical music" presenters, "folk and traditional music" presenters, "jazz" presenters and dozens of others. Since this approach is primarily a variation of the genre approach, it has many of the same strengths and weaknesses. It continues to calcify artistic boundaries; it normalizes particular arts and art forms and marginalizes others. Even those artists and art forms that seek the margins, who explicitly wish to remain outside the "mainstream," create their own stylistic boundaries that admit some styles and leave out others. Once again, who gets to make these distinctions—presenter, artist or audience?

Occasionally, a stylistic or genre approach to presenting centers on the idea of exploring the meanings, the definitions and the boundaries of an art form—its margins as well as its center. Imagine, for example, a series that asks "What is Music?" and contains a range of work that positions the extremes of contemporary music with the more conventional Western European art music. This can be effective for curating a particular performing arts genre because it enables the audience member to experience several artistic styles and develop critical thinking about the genre as a whole. Unfortunately, this curatorial strategy occurs less often than it should. More often, the presenter decides and the audience member accepts, and the questions around the nature of the art form itself are never truly considered. Instead, the audience member simply develops a particularized response to each experience and in this way narrows, rather than expands, his or her aesthetic point of view.

Since art is a cultural definer, it is no longer possible, if it ever was, for a specific genre or style to stake a claim to universality.

A stylistic presenting strategy which asks questions rather than posing givens can be much more interesting and vital. Instead of a "Dance" series, why not a "Is it Dance?" series that explores the margins of the form and raises questions about the art form rather than implying definitive answers.

There is a strong argument to be made for presenters to move dramatically away from the confines of genre and stylistic curating. Presenters can affect how audiences think about art, and it is important that we push those audiences to think about art outside of conventional norms. Well into the postmodern age, artists are pushing against these traditional definitions of their work and exploring the boundaries of what they can do. That alone is justification for presenters to move beyond genre and style as the primary ways of presenting performing arts. Dancers are speaking; singers are moving. Performance has become integrated using dance, theater, music, visual arts, film and video in ways that defy categorization by genre or style.

Beyond artistic practice, the socio-political and cultural environment is also changing in ways that make stylistic and genre demarcations far less relevant. We continue to evolve toward widespread recognition of the multicultural nation that we are and, in fact, always have been. As "outsider" cultures exist next to but refuse to assimilate into a monolithic, generic, Eurocentric culture, the proliferation of diverse performance styles and genres increases exponentially. Since art is a cultural definer, it is no longer possible, if it ever was, for a specific genre or style to stake a claim to universality. As cultural boundaries are simultaneously clarified and blurred, art, which is always culturally specific, responds to the socio-cultural climate. Presenters must choose to either engage in the identity politics of art, narrowing the focus of an art form and correspondingly staking a claim to one center or another, or admit to the chaotic nature of our time and curate series and seasons that reflect that diversity of artistic expression.

Responding to this changed environment creates opportunities for curatorial strategies which, while remaining centered in art, can move beyond genre and style to much more interesting and thought provoking approaches. These strategies can help audiences see art in a different context without completely eliminating artistic boundaries and definitions that remain part of the *lingua franca* of presenters and audiences alike.

The monographic approach is one such possibility. In this, the curator might focus on a single artist and explore multiple aspects of that artist's work. The artist serves as the focal point not only for the performances but also for the contextual activity. The result can be an intellectually and aesthetically interesting exploration of the artist and the work.

Several organizations took such an approach during the Mozart bicentennial in 1991. Organizations from the very largest to the very smallest took the opportunity to create series or whole seasons that explored and illuminated the breadth and depth of Mozart, the man and his work.

Some series were encyclopedic. Lincoln Center embarked on a project to present all of Mozart's work—everything he composed from the fullest opera to ephemeral scraps of composition left lying about. Other organizations created programs focused on the Mozart symphonies, the Mozart piano concertos, the Mozart sonatas, the Mozart chamber music, the Mozart operas. But the creative possibilities for a curatorial strategy were even greater than were often actually produced. Seemingly disparate pieces of music could have been organized around a central idea or theme. One could have explored ideas of death and afterlife in Mozart's chamber music. A series could have focused on Mozart's years in Paris, Salzburg or Vienna, or a series based on humor in Mozart's music or Mozart's personality and how those elements are reflected in his music. Such a series could have used the immensely popular movie *Amadeus* as the springboard for a deeper examination of Mozart's personality and how it appears (or not) in his music. Interestingly, in 2006, in celebration of the 250th anniversary of Mozart's birth, the extraordinary Peter Sellars created a commemorative festival in Vienna, "New Crowned Hope," that contains almost none of Mozart's work. Instead he wants to "pick up where Mozart left off" and present artists whose contemporary work parallels the contemporary circumstance at the time of Mozart's death. What an extraordinary way to celebrate a composer's anniversary and how much more interesting than the retrospective approaches that seem to dominate such an occasion.

A monographic approach to a single choreographer would be an interesting strategy for a dance series. In modern American dance many, perhaps most, companies are driven by a single choreographer, so one strategy might be to produce the same company more than once in a season with each program showing different work and the evolution of the choreographer's vision. There are many mature contemporary choreographers (Bill T. Jones, Merce Cunningham, Mark Morris, Paul Taylor, Trisha Brown, Jawole Willa Jo Zollar, to name a few) for whom this could be an immensely important project, educational as well as popular. Many choreographers have set work on other companies so it is possible to explore the work of one choreographer through multiple companies. It would also be possible to select a single choreographer and, with a range of companies, create a series that explores the artistic influences on that choreographer.

Another curatorial strategy that moves beyond genre and style is a historical approach. This can take several dimensions, the most obvious of which locates the work of a specific period of time. Western European art music organizes itself into relatively rigid historic time periods (baroque, classic, romantic, 20th century), but such a series can become richer if the work is curated with art, dance or theater from the same time period. Selections of pieces can be made based on the art's ability to explicate certain aspects of the historic moment from which it sprang. Is there some key to the seeds of the French revolution in the music and theater of France in the mid- to late-18th century? Does the modern dance created in the 1960s illuminate the social and cultural change occurring at that time? How does music of that time period similarly articulate the essence of that era? Does contemporary art from Latin America or Africa reflect the political turmoil occurring there? What about the African Diaspora and its worldwide influence over multiple centuries and multiple cultures?

Another historical approach can center on a historic moment and then reflect it both backward and forward, looking at previous influences, work prior to a given period and subsequent work. Again, linking the art to the psychology, politics and sociology of the period makes for a much richer result. Significant moments in time which are historic lynchpins (1939 in Europe; 1968 in the United States) can help create broader appreciation and deeper understanding of an art and an era.

One approach often used in playwriting of the 20th century is to deconstruct the art and reinterpret it in light of the contemporary era. We have been given deconstructed Hamlets and Macbeths; why not deconstructed and reinterpreted 18th century music? Why not perform only certain movements of selected pieces by 18th- or 19th-century composers as "new work" for the 20th century? Provocative as this might seem to the classical music lover, think about a series of performances of those sections of Brahms, Beethoven and others that are stylistically akin to work or the 20th century. Placed on a program with 20th century choreographers as well, historicity can be turned inside out and the art is seen for itself and not its period.

The presenter could also select pieces that speak specifically and obviously to contemporary issues and ideas but which were not composed or created in that period. Music, dance and theater that are "classical" are deemed such because of the art's ability to resonate with contemporary audiences, but this is both more and less true of any given work of art. Is it possible to curate a series titled "20th Century Artists" comprised solely of works by artists of the 18th or 19th century, challenging the very idea of historicity? Of course this challenges the presenter and the artists to demonstrate what the links are, but what an exciting experience it could be for audiences and artists!

Another strategy is to curate according to geography or culture—the music of France, the dance of Africa, the theater of China and Japan, the puppetry of Southeast Asia. All these series can and have been presented by organizations throughout the country. Audiences can easily recognize the geographical or cultural focus that connects them to the art. The curator can use that familiarity to present a wide range of artistic styles and genres. This approach allows the presenter to experiment while simultaneously retaining the familiar structure that helps audiences interpret the work. It also gives the presenter greater latitude in choosing the work and the possibility of introducing new forms and ideas to the audience.

Such an approach also provides a broad platform for potential contextualization and makes possible the presentation of less well-known companies and artists who, in and of themselves on a dance or music series, would perhaps not be able to attract much of an audience. When an artist whose vision is important but whose work is not as well known is presented in this way, the work is seen in the context of a larger idea. In this way, the artist gains greater presence for a potential audience. At the same time, the strategy lets the presenter deconstruct preconceived notions about the geography or culture and explicate a fuller view of a place or a people.

The curatorial strategy of thematic programming, which recognizes the importance of a curatorial idea and pushes it to the forefront, can be one of the most potent curatorial strategies that a presenter uses. The presenter decides on a theme for a series or a season and selects performances that illuminate that theme. By centering on an idea or a concept, a presenter offers a series specifically designed to create community discourse. Often the idea is focused in a political or socio-cultural context such as "Crossing Boundaries," "Theater for a New Age," "Cross-cultural Expressions" and other similar ideas. Sometimes the theme is very closely connected to the organization's identity, when a theme is both an organization's aesthetic core and the substance of its curatorial strategy. This is especially evident in presenting organizations that are centered around a cultural identity.

Thematic programming can also occur as a subset of another curatorial strategy. For example, within the genre of jazz programming, a theme might be "Creating Rhythmic Connections." Dozens of large, multidisciplinary presenters curate thematic series titled "New Directions," "New Moves," "New Adventures," "Discovery Series," as thematic approaches to presenting contemporary performance work. Within an historical approach, a theme might be "Contemporary Music: Its Roots in Gospel and Blues." Within a monographic approach, a theme might be subsets of Mozart's work, organized around a particular idea related to his work.

A thematic strategy can serve various functions depending on how the presenter uses it. In some cases, it is little more than a marketing gimmick, a snappy series title under which performances are grouped and the series is sold. In these cases, the theme is often so broad it lacks any real meaning. The theme's role as a marketing tool is arguably important, but it is not necessarily an important curatorial strategy.

Good thematic approaches do more than connect a variety of art and artists; they provoke the audience to think beyond the title. With a theme, the curator demonstrates the desire for the audience to see works of art within a specific context. The theme's purpose is more pronounced when it stimulates new thinking, asks a question or illuminates a new idea for the audience.

Thematic curating requires the presenter to think more deeply and look closely at the nuances of the potential work before moving to the first and most obvious connection or conclusion. A theme can be a question, a thesis, not necessarily self-evident, that at this particular time and place deserves examination and explication through performance. One might look at the creation of a 20th-century city by cultures seemingly in conflict with each other and speculate on its future. Multiculturalism is the reality in America in every community; how can we better understand the complexities of this through a thematically curated series of performances?

Current global ethnic conflicts, balkanization of nations, the rise of religious fundamentalism, and war as solutions to these circumstances are our contemporary realities. These ideas deserve examination, as do many other contemporary conflicts and questions. What are the defining community struggles, events, histories or passions that demand examination through the arts? What can be presented to evoke self-examination and reflection in an entire community? Too often, presenters avoid these opportunities in favor of "presenting great art." In so doing, they marginalize art as a force in contemporary life.

> Good thematic approaches do more than connect a variety of art and artists; they provoke the audience to think beyond the title.

A vital thematic strategy will most often emerge through the presenter's interaction with artists. The presenter, deeply embedded in the particulars of his own situation, may not fully appreciate the larger issues that drive the society and that underpin the work of many artists. Curatorial themes emerge when presenters fully grasp what artists care about. During the culture wars of the 1980s and 1990s, many artists were deeply involved in exploring freedom of expression, the margins of identity and the country's willingness to allow the expressions of those on the margins. In any presenter's community, this may not have been an obvious issue, but for American culture as a whole, it was hugely important. During that time, presenters needed to align with artists in presenting challenging work not only to engage the community in dialogue but also to join with the community in a larger, national dialogue that had profound implications for our culture. Sadly, the dialogue about freedom of expression and the repression of points of view that ran counter to the perceived majority's was seldom actualized as an artistic issue, even if it was seen as a political issue.

Similarly, post 9/11 and with the increasing militarism of the United States, presenters have not necessarily responded immediately by presenting work that critiques a political movement that is deeply problematic. The rise of religious fundamentalism and its proliferation throughout the breadth and depth of American society has barely been challenged, if at all, by presenters in communities where such a theme-based series could have a profound impact. Issues, trends and ideas are important to all communities, no matter how small or isolated. Because the presenter is the one who presents the art, his or her responsibility to be deeply in touch with the larger forces and ideas at work in the world and to create dialogue within the community about those ideas is vitally important.

A drawback to thematic curating becomes evident when the theme becomes either too academic or excessively narrow. While there may certainly be an intellectual validity to the exploration, the range of individuals to whom this speaks may well be too narrow for the organization. This is not to say that thematic programs should only be popular, nor does it preclude a thematic program that speaks profoundly to people already highly invested in the art form. But presenters cannot afford a curatorial self-indulgence any more than an artist can. This is a fine line to negotiate, but the presenter's concern is the connection between art and audience, not simply pursuing one's own artistic interest.

Thematic curating requires a deep understanding of art, community, history, sociology and the politics of place, people and time. It demands a true engagement in the world and in the region within which one works. But the results can be significant in their transformative power, in their educational value and in their ability to assist audiences in seeing art and the world differently than before.

One final art-centered approach is the collage approach. In reviewing season brochures from presenters across the country, we might assume that most presenters use the collage approach, since performances seem to be arranged in what can only be viewed as a random fashion. A collage strategy has an idea behind its apparent randomness. What drives the collage may be a conscious desire to deconstruct purposeful curating as a mechanism for guiding the viewing of art. Instead, the collage approach can juxtapose a variety of art and artists and allow each individual audience member to make whatever connections he or she can by experiencing this apparently random assemblage of art and performance. This approach may be seen as the opposite of the thematic approach (anti-thematic) because it resists any sort of didactic role of the curator, and instead demands that the audience members find their own ways to meaning. The collage approach also makes no attempt at linearity. Contemporary work is aligned with classical work; work from different cultures is juxtaposed with different styles or genres. The presenter's contextualization activities might then be centered around a post-series discussion of what ideas, if any, emerged from this particular assemblage of work.

For the multidisciplinary presenter, such an approach is a *de facto* reality when presenting a body of work and instructing the audience to "choose your own series." Many presenters facilitate this by listing all performances chronologically, as they appear in the season. Regardless of whatever curatorial strategy may or may not be at work, the collage that a given audience member assembles is, from the presenter's perspective, happenstance. A collage curatorial approach, however, carries within it a design that says these events were selected for a coherent reason. They are placed next to each other with the expectation that the spectator will experience them *in toto*, recognize the larger context and develop a response to the collage itself. In the end, collage is neither anarchic nor random, even if it is not designed with such specific intellectual direction as another curatorial strategy might be. Nor does it contain the linear narrative that is often part of other curatorial designs. It is specifically designed to facilitate unexpected encounters and unanticipated reactions, which can be at the heart of a truly vital performance experience.

Thinking about the Audience

Curating from the perspective of the art is a common strategy. Implicit within this approach is a transmitter/receiver paradigm in which the fundamental action is directive, from artist through curator to audience. If, however, the curatorial process is about engaging actively in the issues of audience and interpretation, then the opposite approach, developing curatorial strategies from the perspective of the audience, bears examination as well. This approach begins with understanding the dimensions of the receptive experience and then allows that experience to be the curatorial determinant.

Imagine, for example, a series of performances curated around the idea of eliciting a physical response in the audience. Regardless of genre, style, periodicity, classification of any type, the sole guiding curatorial precept is to center the physical response in the audience. Such a series might include a contemporary music performance whose rhythm and physical set up demands the audience stand and even move throughout the performance. (Imagine a "Gotta Dance!" or

"New Moves" series about the audience dancing and moving, not the artists!) The series might continue with an experimental theater piece in which members of the audience participate in the production or are given the opportunity to participate through a prearranged event. A third performance might be a music ensemble that is experimenting with the physical response of individuals to sound and sound waves. These might all be artists from different backgrounds, histories and performance aesthetics, with the sole unifying factor being their ability to stimulate a physical response in the audience.

Art and artists designed to elicit a particular emotional response in the audience is another curatorial strategy that focuses on the experience of the spectator and audience rather than the art. In this strategy, art is selected primarily for its ability to elicit a specific emotional response. Imagine a series of performances curated around a specific emotion, rage, for example, or joy, and works of art selected that are designed to stimulate that emotion. Certain classical music works do this quite explicitly and could be curated in a series that also features a solo theater piece exploring a single emotion and a dance work similarly focused. Again, imagine a series titled "Cries of the Heart" that refers to the audience's reaction, not the artist's creation.

Direct interaction with the artists, such that the performance cannot occur without the participation of the audience, distinguishes this type of work from the more familiar performance paradigm which separates art and audience.

Yet another curatorial strategy centered in audience response is to create art as an audience's experience, altering the individual's usual response to the art. Rather than providing a vicarious experience of art, the performance would specifically include the audience in the artistic process. Widely understood in the visual arts field as "relational aesthetics" and born out of a dissatisfaction with the commodification of the art world, the idea of such a performance is to contextualize a "real" experience as an art event. Direct interaction with the artists, such that the performance cannot occur without the participation of the audience, distinguishes this type of work from the more familiar performance paradigm which separates art and audience. By redesigning the performance experience as a real experience, the audience member reconsiders a personal relationship to the art and may also reconsider other relationships. In any case, it is the experiential nature of the performance that is the essence of the curatorial strategy.

Curating that is thematic or idea-driven is generally designed to stimulate intellectual thought, expecting the audience to rethink or revisit previously held ideas. This strategy can be taken a step further to curating around a call to action. First, performances are curated around a specific idea, a socio-political construct or rethinking of a particular concept. The performances then are selected not merely to illustrate the idea but also to provoke action on the part of the audience. It may be that the performances address a particular social injustice and are designed to seek an immediate, active response from the audience. The performance becomes as much about taking action as it is about learning or viewing from a distance. The series can focus around the ramifications of an idea or a philosophy and have the call to action embedded in the work of the artists. An example could be a series devoted to social justice in the United States. A thematic series might present several performances of artists of various backgrounds, exploring their aesthetic and cultural differences as they emerge in the artistic process. But a series designed to elicit a response in an audience might select artists and work that both illustrate social injustices and contain as part of the performance a call to action to address them. Again, the key difference is in the idea behind the curatorial strategy. This is a strategy for organizations that see themselves as committed to social change.

All of these curatorial strategies have their own value and any can serve as the foundation of a presenter's work or of an organization's commitment to the presenting endeavor. In practice, presenters will mix many of these strategies in any given series—curating by genre while still exploring a theme or idea, creating a monographic approach that elucidates new ideas and causes a specific emotional response in an audience, and dozens of other such combinations. Regardless of the approach, the important point is that the presenter's work as curator is intentional. Pushing one's thinking to embrace curatorial ideas, roles and strategies insures that the program created begins to approach the potential complexity and richness of performing arts presenting.

Before leaving this section, I want to acknowledge again the reality that as a curator, the presenter can only select, arrange and contextualize the work of artists. He or she does not create the work. This being the case, presenters do not have an unlimited universe of choices available to them around which they can create a program that fully explicates the curatorial idea that they believe is most important right now for their communities. Add to this the limitations of budgets, availability of the artists, technical requirements, scheduling and the host of other issues that are the daily headaches of a presenter and the idea that a presenter might select a role, a strategy, an idea and have the artistic resources available to enact that idea seems daunting indeed. And it is, no question. Certainly in the curatorial process we will constantly be required to rethink, restructure and revise the programs that we are creating. That too however, is part of what makes being a presenter both enriching and challenging. The difficulties of the work simply require that we become more creative and better at our work as we approach each successive curatorial project.

The difficulty of the task should not stop us from pursuing it with all of the energy, enthusiasm and passion that we can. As professionals in the field we must strive always to accomplish the highest and most challenging of our goals, creating great work on behalf of our organizations, our communities and even ourselves. Nothing less should be acceptable.

CONCLUSION

I HAVE TRIED TO ARTICULATE IN THIS BOOK WHAT I BELIEVE IS THE BASIS OF THE PERFORMING arts presenter's work. I hope these ideas will encourage presenters to begin thinking differently about the profession of performing arts presenting. We begin with an understanding of the performance experience—what can happen when art, artist and audience connect—and we accept responsibility for building that experience. Seeing the performance in its larger context enables us to also understand our role as creators of meaning and as sites of cultural discourse. Through the curatorial process, we make the important decisions about how ideas are made manifest. These decisions on behalf of our organizations and our community profoundly shape our culture.

Historically, the "real work" of the presenter has been thought to be about the concrete realities of decision-making around seasons, schedules, budgets and boards, and this remains very much the case. In no way do I seek to diminish the importance of this work and of the presenter's ability to accomplish these tasks. Inexperience, mistakes and missteps in logistics have caused no end of difficulties for presenting organizations, some of which have contracted and even died when the presenter, staff and/or board were ill equipped to carry out the organization's work.

But no presenting organization has soared to greatness on the basis of details and logistics. No presenting organization has transformed the community, the nation or the world without boldly embracing the full breadth and depth of our work. Without vision, without passion for the deepest, most important challenges of presenting, the presenting endeavor is ultimately without meaning.

Finally, I return to the concept of an arts ecology and our role as presenters in it. Beyond creating seasons and putting on performances, it is clear that the presenter has a far more important role to play in that ecology. Thoughtful curating, contextualizing the art, engaging the community, shaping the cultural discourse—this is what actually comprises the work of the presenter.

In the end, not only art matters. Presenting matters. In our role as shapers of culture, we have the opportunity to profoundly affect not just the arts ecology but also the world we live in. Presenting is more than a career or a profession, it is a calling. Like any calling, it presents us with challenges, difficulties, obstacles and frustrations. But it also can provide us with great rewards and incredible gratification. It is work that is both worth doing and worth caring about. Only through our best efforts can we succeed in our work and provide cultural leadership in a changing world.

BIBLIOGRAPHY

IN WORKING ON THIS PROJECT I LOOKED FOR PUBLICATIONS ABOUT CURATING THE performing arts. Of which I found nothing. Search "performing arts curating" in amazon.com and 3 books come up—one on marketing, one on degree programs and the Art Director's Annual. Google the phrase. and one entry comes up, a graduate architecture program at a school in London. Google "performing arts presenting" and a mere 624 entries come up, most of then press releases about grant awards to presenting organizations. There is clearly a dearth of literature in our field.

I did, however, find some edited collections on curating in the visual arts which were quite helpful and which are listed here.

For the rare presenter who has not read *An American Dialogue*, I include it here. It is a foundational source for any performing arts presenter.

Greenberg, Reesa, Bruce W. Ferguson, Sandy Nairne, eds. *Thinking about Exhibitions*. New York: Routledge, 1996.

Hager, Mark A. and Thomas H. Pollak. *The Capacity of Performing Arts Presenting Organizations*. Washington, D.C.: The Urban Institute, 2002.

Kuoni, Carin, ed. *Words of Wisdom: A Curator's Vade Mecum on Contemporary Art*. New York: Independent Curators International, 2001.

McDaniel, Nello and George Thorn. *The Workpapers One; Rethinking and Restructuring the Arts Organization*. New York: FEDAPT,1990.

National Task Force on Presenting and Touring the Performing Arts. *An American Dialogue*. Washington, D.C.: The Association of Performing Arts Presenters, 1989.

Sherman, Daniel J. and Irit Rogoff, eds. *Museum Culture: Histories, Discourse and Spectacles*. Minneapolis: University of Minnesota Press, 1994.

Wade, Gavin, ed. *Curating in the 21st Century*. Walsall, United Kingdom: University of Wolverhampton, 2000.

ACKNOWLEDGEMENTS

THIS BOOK IS THE PRODUCT OF 20-PLUS YEARS OF WORK IN THE PRESENTING FIELD. During that time, professional colleagues and friends who are too numerous to list here, have contributed to my development as a presenter and thus have informed the contents of this book. I am especially indebted to the members of the various presenter consortia I belonged to—Rocky Mountain Arts Consortium, Illinois Presenter Network, PA Presenters, Arizona Presenter's Alliance, California Presenters, Major University Presenters, Contemporary Arts Centers, The African Contemporary Arts Consortium—for creating a forum for sharing ideas and including me in that conversation.

There are some people, however, whom I must thank for generously sharing their own particular knowledge and expertise with me, often at crucial moments in my career. My deepest thanks then to Marc Baylin, Lisa Booth, Linda Brumbach, Marlu Burkamp, Janet Cowperthwaite, Carolelinda Dickey, Sue Endrizzi, Ellis Finger, Olga Garay, Kathy Hotchner, Bill T. Jones, John Dale Kennedy, Maurine Knighton, Liz Lerman, Pamela McKean, Rob Mickelsen, Tim Miller, Bill Mitchell, Harold Norris, Cleo Parker Robinson, Ann Rosenthal, David Rousseve, Peter Sellars, Marna Seltzer, Linda Shelton, Mikki Shepard, Andrea Snyder, Dean Stein, Ivan Sygoda, Jed Wheeler and Cathy Zimmerman for shaping my thinking about the presenting field.

Special thanks to James Moeser, who took a big risk when he hired me at Penn State in 1987 and became an incomparable mentor and friend. My thinking about several of the ideas articulated here began when I was in that position. In 1994, I moved to the University of Arizona and without question my experience there guided the writing of this book. Vice President Saunie Taylor was an extraordinary individual to work for and arranged for me to have a summer sabbatical so I could write the first draft. Simply stated, the book would never have happened without her. I will always be grateful to Saunie and the University of Arizona for supporting my work. All of my colleagues there, especially Mark Rasdorf and Ed Brown, deserve special thanks for teaching me and for keeping the organization going while I researched and wrote the book.

My service on the Board of the Association of Performing Arts Presenters from 1993 to 2003 was invaluable and I owe the organization a huge debt of gratitude. Through Arts Presenters, I was blessed to meet and know an incredibly gifted group of fellow board members from around the country who constantly challenged me with their sophisticated thinking and their commitment to the field. Susie Farr gave me the chance to be an instructor for "The Basic," where, working with Fran Holden and others, I began to crystallize my thinking about the field of performing arts presenting. Tony Tapia asked me to rewrite the curriculum, an exercise which served as the real beginning of this project. I taught the course several times in several places and learned from the dozens of students with whom I came into contact, but especially from co-instructors Pam Green, Phyllis Brzozowska, Margaret Lawrence, Dawn Gibson-Brehon and others. Sincere thanks to all of them. I am especially grateful to Sandra Gibson and Patrick Madden for believing in the book and working to get it out to the field.

By 2003, I had a first draft that I circulated to several colleagues. I'm grateful to Liz Lerman, Jed Wheeler, David Gere, Tom Wolf, Gerry Yoshitomi and Kim Chan for their willingness to read and comment on early drafts. Ivan Sygoda in his usual meticulous fashion went through the text line by line and made brilliant rhetorical and content suggestions. Mikki Shepard spent an entire afternoon with me, discussing and rethinking nearly all of the ideas in the book, an extraordinary gift. Albert Pertalion urged me to write more clearly and pushed me to get it out to the field quickly. Jana Richman did the first edit of the manuscript and commiserated with me daily about the anxieties of the writing process. Romalyn Tilghman and Joël Tan also reviewied the manuscript and provided further clarity and inspiration. Thanks to Arts Presenters, Suzanne G. Fox did the final editing and, in addition to cleaning up my prose, made me think again about some of my assertions. Her challenges to me are reflected in the final manuscript which is, I believe, markedly better for her intervention. Thanks to all of them.

I thank my family, and especially my parents, Bud and Phyllis Foster, for instilling in me the not always fashionable idea that I could do anything if I put my mind to it. My sister Leslie continues to give me extraordinary support, personally and professionally. Kathy Poirier made my career possible by steadfastly and lovingly supporting every new direction I chose to pursue, whatever the personal cost to her and our children. I can never fully account to her for that. My two sons, Aaron and Brandon, were willingly, and sometimes not so willingly, dragged to every conceivable performance in my pursuit of art. While my career provoked a life of frequent absence from them, it also produced extraordinary experiences of our mutual engagement with art and artists. Thanks, boys.

Finally, I dedicate this book with great love and enormous respect to my life partner, Nayan Shah, who believed even before I did that I could and should write this book and made it seem the most natural thing in the world that I would. He never wavered from that conviction, even when I did. During my sabbatical, I wrote the first draft at his home in San Diego under his strong, loving care. With Nayan, I have learned that second acts in life are not only possible, but can be truly extraordinary.

San Francisco
September, 2006